NEW
THINKING
ALLOWED
DIALOGUES

NEW THINKING ALLOWED DIALOGUES

UFOs and UAP: Are we Really Alone?

JEFFREY MISHLOVE

www.whitecrowbooks.com

New Thinking Allowed Dialogues: UFOs and UAP: Are we Really Alone?

This compilation, Copyright © 2024 by New Thinking Allowed Foundation.
All rights reserved.
Published by New Thinking Allowed, an imprint of White Crow Productions Ltd.

The right of Jeffrey Mishlove to be identified as the author of this work has been
asserted by him in accordance with the Copyright, Design and Patents act 1988.

A CIP catalogue record for this book is available from the British Library.

For information, contact White Crow Books by
e-mail: info@whitecrowbooks.com.

Cover Design by Jana Rogge & Astrid@Astridpaints.com
Interior design by Velin@Perseus-Design.com

Paperback: ISBN: 978-1-78677-242-8
eBook: ISBN: 978-1-78677-243-5

Non Fiction / Body, Mind & Spirit / UFOs &
Extraterrestrials / Parapsychology /

ESP, Clairvoyance, Precognition, Telepathy.

www.whitecrowbooks.com

Contents

A Note from Jeff

While most readers are aware of the current public discussions concerning UFOs/UAP, not so many realize that this has been a hot topic for as long as I can remember. As a 10-year-old child, in the mid-1950s, for example, I was already reading all the UFO books that I could find in the local library (which was rather well-stocked)—and even writing letters to the authors. In fact, I received a reply from noted UFO skeptic of that era, Donald Menzel, Director of the Harvard University Observatory, who made a point of assuring me that UFOs did not really exist.

In the 1970s, as I began my academic work in the field of parapsychology, the Israeli psychic Uri Geller was achieving global fame. His biographer, Andrija Puharich, made a point of vividly describing the connections between a variety of UFO-type encounters and Uri's ostensible psychokinetic abilities. I was able to verify the validity of one such UFO appearance involving Geller by interviewing one of the witnesses, journalist Ila Ziebel.

From my perspective, the connection between UFOs and psychokinetic manifestations was amply illustrated in the case of Ted Owens, who called himself "the PK Man." Few events in my life have been more dramatic than the UFO appearance over Sonoma State College on December 8, 1976, which was witnessed simultaneously by hundreds of individuals with cameras on the ground, as well as by a pilot flying 3,000 feet above the campus. A photograph of that event was published on the front page of the *Berkeley Gazette*.

Only a few days before, Owens had told me during an animated phone call that he was about to "produce" a UFO that would be photographed and that the photo would be published on the front page of a local Bay Area newspaper. As a result of this experience, and others, I have been indelibly impressed with the connection between UFOs and parapsychology. Of course, in those days, neither parapsychologists nor UFOlogists were eager to pursue this connection. In fact, one noted parapsychologist withdrew from my dissertation committee at the University of California because he objected to my interest in UFOlogy.

All this controversy has made UFO/UAP phenomena difficult to study or understand. More than half a century since my first inquiries, the subject remains among the greatest mysteries facing humankind. For this reason, I am very grateful to have been able to conduct in-depth interviews with leading experts in this field. Now, I am even more grateful to be able to share these conversations with a reading audience.

This book has been made possible because of a team of volunteer editors and designers working with the New Thinking Allowed Foundation. They include Greta Peavy, Emmy Vadnais, Laura Neubert, Elizabeth Lord, and Jana Rogge.

We have worked diligently to make sure that the spoken words from our interviews will flow smoothly on the written pages of a book. This book can be considered a window into the minds of some of the most respected researchers in the field of UFOlogy.

An additional acknowledgment, of course, is due to our fearless publisher, Jon Beecher, of White Crow Books who is working with us closely to establish the *New Thinking Allowed Dialogues* imprint.

Preface

⌒

Bob Davis, Ph.D.

My journey in this arena stands as a testament to intellectual curiosity. As a professor and researcher in the neuro-sensory sciences, and "closet ufologist" within the halls of academia for over three decades, I have researched the literature and events surrounding Unidentified Aerial Phenomena (UAP) since the 1960s. Collectively, the diverse contributions of authorities such as astronomer, J. Allen Hynek, astronaut and founder of the Institute of Noetic Sciences, Edgar Mitchell, psychiatrist and alien abduction researcher, John E. Mack, and computer scientist and legendary researcher Jacques Vallée, has helped me to navigate the complexities of this phenomenon with a comprehensive understanding, bringing together scientific scrutiny, noetic exploration, psychiatric insights, and analytical rigor with a broad scope, and as logically as possible. But logic, the stalwart companion of scientific inquiry, often falters in the face of the paranormal. In the past few post-retirement years, however, I have defied the constraints of the ordinary, embarking on a dedicated journey to bridge the gap between scientific inquiry and the exploration of extraordinary experiences.

This effort resulted in a published study, "A Study on Reported Contact with Non-Human Intelligence Associated with Unidentified Aerial Phenomena" (*Journal of Scientific Exploration*, Vol 32: 2018), and three books: *The UFO Phenomenon: Should I Believe* (2015); *Life After Death: An Analysis of the Evidence* (2017); and *Unseen Forces: The integration of Science, Reality and You* (2019). And, now, I am co-producing "The Consciousness Connection" (consciousnessfilm.info); a documentary weaving the threads of science, consciousness, and the unexplained, with leading research scientists and paranormal experiencers, including legendary host and producer of the *New Thinking Allowed* channel on YouTube, and author of the *New Thinking Allowed Dialogues*, Jeffrey Mishlove, Ph.D. This film will attempt to enrich our collective understanding of the mysterious realms where science, consciousness, and the unexplained entwine.

Jeffrey Mishlove, a luminary in parapsychology and consciousness studies, emerges as a beacon of intellectual exploration in the realm of the paranormal. His commitment to fostering dialogue and understanding, particularly in the context of UAP for this book, is illustrated through his impressive interviews with notable participants, orchestrating intellectual discussions in various media platforms, as represented in this book. In unique Mishlove style, he masterfully crafts questions, sculpting the narrative with precision to ensure accuracy, clarity, and depth of discussion, which serves not only as an educational tool, but also as a catalyst for unraveling the intricacies of the paranormal. His interviews and this book become a portal, inviting curious minds to explore the uncharted territories where consciousness and the paranormal meet.

Throughout this book, common UAP themes emerge, ranging from national security intelligence and disinformation campaigns, interactions with UAP and paranormal activity, and the enigmatic concept of consciousness. The focal point on the UAP, and the diverse array of researchers and experiencers from varied academic and professional backgrounds, unfolds as a testament to the interdisciplinary nature of and associated perspectives of how the UAP is addressed. From professional backgrounds ranging from religious studies, philosophy, metaphysics, aerospace, law, to computer science, discussions traverse the controversial landscape of religious and cultural influences, legal, psychological, philosophical, and metaphysical concerns, and government transparency. This juxtaposition of perspectives, influenced by individual beliefs, personalities, and professional backgrounds, serve as a foundation upon which the UAP is perceived in this comprehensive treatment of this phenomenon.

One such perspective is evidenced in the work of philosopher, metaphysician, and Sufi Muslim, Charles Upton, who offers a unique dimension to this book's eclectic collection of interviews. In his book *UFOs and the Demonic*, and interview with Mishlove, Upton challenges the conventional view of the UAP myth as a series of individual encounters, postulating it as a profound challenge to established belief systems. Through his philosophical lens, the UAP becomes not just a phenomenon but also a calculated assault on religion itself, suggesting that non-human entities are orchestrating a replacement of the "divine creator" through genetic engineering. Upton's interpretation is supported in his reframing of the alien abduction phenomenon, presenting an alternative perspective to the benevolent encounters discussed by John E. Mack. Upton aligns the UAP with ancient religious narratives, weaving a narrative that places it within the realm of demons, existing in the delicate balance between the material and the metaphysical.

Charles Upton's alluded "realm," presents a broad challenge to established belief systems—one that may be the same experienced by all who report to interact with the phenomenon, including noted fiction and non-fiction author, Whitley Strieber. Strieber, the author of *Communion: A True Story*, is a pivotal figure in the intricate web of UAP abduction narratives. His literary skills extend beyond the realms of traditional storytelling, offering a deeply personal account that transcends the boundaries of conventional existence. In Strieber's narrative, he weaves tales of physical and telepathic interactions with non-human entities, encounters with artificial alien implants, and even communication with his deceased wife. The vivid imagery he paints captures the intensity and uniqueness of his believed range of paranormal experiences, complete with physical scars and the transformative emotional odyssey that unfolded over time. Strieber extends an invitation to transcend the confines of conventional understanding, urging readers to explore new ontological dimensions. While the validity of such accounts, even when presented by seemingly well-balanced individuals like Strieber, remains a subject of debate within the broader dialogue on the phenomenon, his influence on the popularization of alien abduction stories and the wide-ranging discourse on UAP cannot be denied.

In the exchange between Jeffrey Mishlove and prominent scholar known for his work in the fields of religion and philosophy, Jeffrey Kripal, the spotlight on Whitley Strieber's experiences and their collaborative work, *The Supernatural: A New Vision of the Unexplained*, becomes a pivotal point for exploring experiences that extend beyond the confines of conventional understanding, having broader implications for understanding the paranormal within the context of UAP. Mishlove cleverly weaves Strieber's paranormal experiences into the mix, whose friend Kripal, finds challenging to explain. Drawing from his philosophical background, unexplained personal experiences, and particularly those of Whitley Strieber, Kripal advocates for the development of a cultural theory of imagination. He emphasizes the importance of recognizing the imagination as a foundational element for understanding how it serves as a key conceptual tool to help bridge the gap between the material and the spiritual or paranormal dimensions for understanding experiences that defy traditional classification. During their discussion, Mishlove's reference to his book, *The PK Man*, adds a layer of gravitas to the exploration of this phenomenon. This work, based on a decade-long case study with Ted Owens, showcases demonstrations of psychokinetic abilities and hints at a potential telepathic connection with non-human beings, paralleling the experiences detailed by Strieber. Mishlove's serious consideration of these phenomena, as evidenced by his study, aligns with the gravity of Strieber's experiences and Kripal's philosophical inquiry.

The themes of paranormal activity and metaphysics, written about by Strieber and Kripal, is also addressed by remote viewer, Daz Smith. The discussion with Smith centers on the book *Penetration* by Ingo Swann, which underscores the multifaceted nature of enigmatic experiences surrounding UAP. Smith, influenced by the insights of remote viewer, Ingo Swann, who claimed to have unraveled the layers of telepathic communication with non-human entities on this and other planets, casts light on the deeper dimensions of these encounters. Smith's exploration of remote viewing, coupled with his experiences and belief in a controlling force or non-human entity beyond the scope of human understanding, adds a layer of complexity to the broader discourse on UAP. It suggests a common force beneath the symbolic narratives presented by various contributors in this book.

The revelations by Nick Cook, aerospace journalist and author of *The Hunt for Zero Point: Inside the Classified World of Antigravity Technology*, and Gregory Bishop, investigative author of *Project Beta: The Story of Paul Bennewitz, National Security, and the Creation of a Modern UFO Myth*, showcase the intricate maneuvers of government agencies to shape narratives, divert attention, and safeguard classified military projects to protect sensitive information in the creation of a modern UAP lore. Bishop's exploration into the events surrounding Paul Bennewitz's UAP-related investigations in the late 1970s and early 1980s, unveils the extent to which authorities controlled the evolving UAP myth using a web of disinformation for their own purposes. Bishop recounts how Bennewitz's genuine belief in discovering evidence of extraterrestrial activity near Kirtland Air Force Base became entangled in a narrative manipulated by government agencies that fed him disinformation to control the narrative. Like Bishop, Cook also sheds light on the intricate interplay within the secretive world of government, emphasizing the cloak-and-dagger nature of UAP research. His exploration of UAP-related technologies extends beyond mere sightings and encounters as he delves into the realm of speculative and often classified aerospace research, seeking to understand whether there is a connection between advanced propulsion systems developed by the military and the unconventional flight characteristics reported in UAP sightings. Cook emphasizes the urgency surrounding potential technological applications of UAP-related discoveries among world powers, and the broader societal responsibility associated with these advancements, extending beyond the realms of aerospace and defense, and the complex interplay behind the world of government secrecy of the phenomenon. Both Bishop and Cook suggest that there is a hidden and secretive dimension to how government agencies handle and manage information related to this phenomenon.

Prominent Federal Civil Rights Attorney Daniel Sheehan's extensive involvement in significant cases over the last fifty years, as detailed in his book *The People's Advocate: The Life and Legal History of America's Most Fearless Public Interest Lawyer*, underscores his dedication to public interest, justice and advocacy. He has also chosen to speak publicly about UAP and alien visitation and by actively participating in the New Paradigm Institute to undertake investigations of UAP incidents. In doing so, he now extends his legal and investigative expertise to a realm that has garnered increased attention in recent times. In his revealing discussion with Mishlove, his personal accounts of photographic evidence from the Roswell incident and Project Blue Book, and references to government crash retrieval and reverse engineering programs, highlights the depth of his knowledge and engagement with historical UAP-related activities. The revelation of secret CIA programs aimed at undermining the careers of UAP whistle-blowers and the discussion of recent legislative efforts for greater disclosure, emphasize Sheehan's commitment to shedding light on these phenomena. His contention that the Department of Defense is not openly sharing information with the public but rather trying to establish dominance over the planet through back-engineering UFO technology adds a provocative dimension surrounding UAP. Beyond technological military-related research, Sheehan claims knowledge of secret programs within both the Pentagon and the CIA and extends to the relationship between consciousness and the UFO phenomena. In response to what he sees as a lack of transparency, Sheehan plans to utilize subpoena power and establish an independent panel to review and obtain all the information that the U.S. government has regarding UAP, advocating for transparency, disclosure, and an independent review of government-held information on the matter.

Jacques Vallée, a legendary UAP researcher and the author of influential books such as *Trinity: The Best Kept Secret, The Invisible College,* and *Passport to Magonia,* brings a unique perspective that resonates with the themes expressed by all interviewees in this book. Vallée sees UAP not merely as isolated phenomena but as manifestations of a broader and more intricate reality. Drawing on his academic background in computer sciences, Vallée offers a meticulous examination of historical collections of UAP database files and shares his frustration at the current lack of interest and analysis of this valuable information, advocating for a disciplined scientific rigor in UAP research. In his critique, Vallée points out the potential oversight in current research methodologies and the importance of distinguishing the behavior of UAP over a nuclear base versus over military or commercial aircraft. These performance nuances, according to Vallée, represent just one variable, among others, that should be considered in the analysis of existing UAP database files spanning the last five decades. He urges researchers to adopt a comprehensive approach, and underscores the importance of integrating scientific rigor in understanding the physical aspects of the phenomenon while simultaneously considering broader metaphysical dimensions. In doing so, Vallée echoes the sentiments expressed by others interviewed in this book, emphasizing the need for a holistic exploration to better understand the nature and meaning of UAP encounters.

Throughout the book, it becomes evident that the paranormal theme serves as a lens through which its contributors attempt to make sense of the mysterious and often perplexing occurrences associated with UAP. Upton's consideration of the demonic, Kripal's exploration of the metaphysical or imaginal realm, Vallee's proposition of metaphysical dimensions, Smith's contemplation of a controlling force, and Strieber's personal journey involving non-human interactions, introduces a unique flavor to the discourse, reflecting the complexity inherent in the phenomenon.

Another prevalent thread that weaves through these diverse perspectives is the idea that an aspect of consciousness underlies the phenomenon. Whether it is conceptualized as a demonic force, a metaphysical realm, or a controlling entity, the influence of consciousness is a common denominator—one reinforced by Sheehan's knowledge of secret programs within the Pentagon and CIA regarding consciousness and the phenomena. This shared observation suggests a profound connection between the UAP and the human mind, leaving readers with challenging ideas to contemplate.

The book's mastery lies in its comprehensive exploration of the varied lenses through which people approach the subject, reflecting the richness and complexity of the phenomenon itself. And based on its content, it seems at this point in our evolutionary and intellectual development, we can only speculate if the phenomenon represents a co-existing native, extraterrestrial, or interdimensional life form, capable of mitigating gravity and inertia, purposeful intent, and human interaction surrounding UAP. The recognition that the answers may elude us or may even be beyond our current conceptual frameworks adds an element of humility to the pursuit of this knowledge.

The invitation to reconsider and expand our ontological understanding of existence is a powerful takeaway from the book. It suggests that the UA phenomenon, regardless of its true nature, challenges our foundational beliefs about the nature of reality. This call to expand our intellectual and philosophical horizons encourages a broader and more inclusive approach to understanding existence.

In summary, the book is a valuable and revealing contribution, presenting timely and pertinent scholarly information in a thought-provoking manner. Its exploration of the UA phenomenon not only delves into the intricacies of the subject matter but also serves as a catalyst for broader reflections on the nature of existence itself.

1

The New Era in UFO Research
with
Jacques Vallée

⌇

Jeffrey Mishlove: Our topic today is the new era in UFO research. My guest is the legendary UFO researcher, Jacques Vallée. He is the author of numerous books including *Passport to Magonia, The Invisible College, Messengers of Deception, Forbidden Science* in four volumes, *Wonders in the Sky, Confrontations: A Scientist's Search for Alien Contact, Dimensions: A Casebook of Alien Contact, Revelations: Alien Contact and Human Deception,* and most recently, *Trinity: The Best Kept Secret.* Jacques is based in the San Francisco region. Welcome, Jacques. It's nice to be with you once again.

Jaques Vallée: Good to see you, Jeffrey.

Mishlove: You were in Paris, when we spoke last, about to attend a major international meeting of UFO researchers and government officials from around the world. It seemed to me at the time, and I think to you as well, that this meeting was in effect inaugurating a new era in the field of UFO research.

Vallée: There were eight nations represented and this is something that we rarely hear people talking about in the United States. We're so dominated by the American media that we tend to forget that this research has been going on around the world for a very long time. Every country is following the subject, some intensely. Some go through periods of being very interested in it and doing research and then periods where they tend to give up for a while, and then the interest reawakens. For example, Argentina.

In the US, people are only interested in what America does. It's true that it dominates the news and that there are so many competing media outlets in the US that UFO information rarely gets to the surface for people to hear about it. It's a little harder even in France for a scientist to remain aware of what the observations are at any given time. But there is a good network of amateur UFO organizations that cover different parts of the country. The French have not instituted military control of UFO information like the US has. In the US, essentially, the Pentagon has always controlled the news about UFOs, either through the Air Force, through the Navy, or now through the new organization that has been set up, which is good. But most of the reports that, as a scientist, I want to study, are civilian reports, which are not classified. They may not involve high technology, but they do involve people experiencing a phenomenon and that's really the root of the issue for scientists. That's where we have to start.

In France, the government agency that is in charge of gathering the information and studying it is the French equivalent of NASA, the CNES (Centre National D'Etudes Spatiales or The National Center for Space Studies). I've been privileged to serve on a scientific review panel at CNES for the last six years. We follow the most interesting reports that, at various levels, have not been explained. It's a very rewarding place from which to study the phenomenon because it has been reviewed by pretty much every scientific discipline along the way. It's a small group, but it has access to all the resources, not only of CNES, but also of the research organizations, the medical organizations, and so on. It has been in existence for forty years, and I don't think people know about that in the US.

Mishlove: You mentioned there were eight countries there, so France would be one example, but I know UFO sightings are reported in every country, pretty much.

Vallée: There are reports from every country that are followed, not necessarily on a regular basis by every country. Holland was there—they're very interested—Norway, Sweden, and Germany. Spain of course has compiled files on the subject for a long time. We've been exchanging data across Europe. Argentina was represented via a teleconferencing link. Conferences like this make for a very rich discussion. It went on for three days. It was not public, but all the organizations that are doing credible private research were there. It was not just a bunch of government people and there was nothing classified.

Mishlove: I assume that the US government, as far as I can tell, seems to have abandoned its policy of debunking UFO sightings and ridiculing UFO witnesses and contactees; that will have a big impact on the global search for understanding about UFOs.

Vallée: Yes, and I'm very hopeful. I think it's a new phase and I'm very grateful to be here to see it. I am in reasonably good health to continue my work and, hopefully, to exchange data, if called upon, with people who are running those new projects. As you know, I've been working with them all along and we know each other. But the government has its own structure and its own need to do things in a certain way, especially regarding the Pentagon. It's a third phase. It's not formal, but I roughly organize the history into three major phases.

From 1945 to the Condon Report in 1967-68, we have mainly the Air Force taking an interest in this. The Air Force was charged with the responsibility to gather the reports, but they gathered them from the public, from their own pilots, or from other branches of the government, like the Navy. It was different from what's going on now. The Air Force was really looking at the whole spectrum and they tried to do a good job within their structure. Sometimes it was very good and sometimes it was, frankly, mediocre. Then in 1967, there was the Condon study that resulted in the *New York Times* broadcasting to the world that there was no scientific value in studying UFOs.

The second phase was very dark. It lasted from 1967 to very recently. Of course, the research continued in spite of the *New York Times*, in spite of the Condon Report, in spite of the Academy of Sciences, because people continued to see things. They were not being looked at from a scientific or from a rational viewpoint; there were all kinds of extrapolations. The military continued to study UFOs because they were showing up on their radar. The only difference is that *The New York Times* didn't know about it and only the people who were paying attention and doing research, particularly in Silicon Valley, were following it from a technology perspective. NASA knew about it, except that nobody was officially talking about it and there was only private research funding. There are a few groups, like MUFON, that did an extraordinarily good job of continuing to talk to witnesses, publish their reports and to build databases, as I did.

The third phase starts now and we really don't know what's going to happen. I think it's very encouraging that Congress has taken the initiative in forcing openness, but openness is not disclosure. Everybody wants disclosure, but nobody has told us what they mean by that. What is there to disclose? If we don't know what those things are, there can be no disclosure. What we have is a disclosure that there is a phenomenon we don't understand. I think in the United States—unless you've been buried in a dark room with no TV—you probably know that there is something going on that has not been solved by the Academy of Sciences, and has been kept very quiet by the military all these years. I don't believe in disclosure that much, but I do believe in openness. Hopefully, we will open the doors and the windows and let people come forward with their information.

Mishlove: As I recall, it was in 1954 or so. There was, I think I have the name correct, the Robertson panel that argued that the government should try to dismiss interest in UFOs. There was concern that if people thought the government wasn't in control of things, that would create widespread panic and that should be avoided.

Vallée: That was part of it. That panel, by the way, was top secret. What the people were told, and then what you find in UFO books, is that, eventually, part of the information was revealed. The panel had taken place, and they had recommended dismissing most of the reports from the public because they were too vague. On the contrary, they thought there should be more intense attention placed on it by the Pentagon to try to get better data, which sounds reasonable given the times. Now we know it wasn't enough.

To some extent that's what's going to happen now. There is a group that is very much within the military structure that has been tasked with looking at the military reports because they have sensor data, aircraft data, spectral analysis, radar images, and infrared images. They have all that, and they have the tools and the budget to analyze it. The military has already said that they will only look at the best-described and measured data, which is about two percent of all the reports. The question that any scientist would ask is: what are you going to do with the other ninety-eight percent?

I'm interested in the other ninety-eight percent because a farmer in their field has a pretty good sense of their environment, especially since animals react to UFOs. People see them for minutes or hours, and we can get very good human data from that. We don't get all the scientific data we would like to get, but maybe that will lead to a new generation of sensors we can develop. That's what Mr. Robert Bigelow and the project in Nevada was trying to do. It's a good idea.

The other part of the Robertson panel was a lot more dark, and it has since come out in little bits and pieces. I have discussed it with Professor J. Allen Hynek, who was present many times. He testified before the panel though he was not there for every meeting. I also spoke to the man who was in charge of photographic intelligence for the Pentagon at the time. He was in charge of the classified films and the photographs, and he presented those to the panel. They reviewed all the data for several days. These people there were the luminaries of American science with classified access—above top secret—for their work, not just for the panel. So they knew how to handle that kind of data.

The real concern was a potential nuclear attack from the Soviet Union, which, in those days, was something to be considered. Not that we don't have to consider it now, but in those days that was really the number one scenario to watch for. The Air Force relied on the network of teletypes because there was no Internet and the phone system couldn't be used effectively to get that kind of data. Those teletypes could be saturated from all the different organizations within the network reporting fake UFOs, and preventing communication at the top level needing to respond to a nuclear attack. That was the real assignment the panel had. The assignment did not come from the Air Force. That was a lie. It came from the Central Intelligence Agency.

After my PhD in AI from Northwestern University, during the summer, Dr. Hynek said it would be a great idea to reorganize his files. They were very disorganized, went back many years and had never been restructured. I had an office in the computation center where I was working full time then. I went out and bought some filing cabinets, then started going through all the files, which included those from the Air Force. I spent four years reorganizing and reducing them to computer files, and then sorting to find the real cases from the cases that could be explained. I still have that data.

I hear that one of the things that the new panel is going to do is to review old files as ordered by congress. I spent four years with the help of my wife, who was a professional psychologist, [to] get the access to Hynek, to the Air Force data and Major Quintanillo. We used the resources of the university to segregate the twenty percent of the data that had to do with UFOs and threw out the other eighty percent, which were misperceptions, misclassifications and so on. We spent four years reviewing each month at a time, for the totality of Project Bluebook. Nobody has bothered to review those files that are in machine-readable form. That's only one of the databases we have. I'd be happy to donate it to the new guys in charge if they are interested, or they can redo it themselves. I don't think Congress realizes how much work is involved just with that one source of data.

The Robertson panel data was in Hynek's files and he knew it was there. He had not released it to the public since 1954 because everybody was disgusted with the conclusions that essentially closed off a lot of the scientific interest in the data. What Dr. Hynek and I wanted was to get American scientists to start looking at the data. The Robertson panel was a setback because they said only the military has the right sensors to get good data, which is partly true. But then they threw out ninety percent of pertinent information, which included all the medical impact, and the open-air data.

I went through the files and restructured them. I hit upon a little folder that everybody had forgotten, especially Dr. Hynek. It had two pages from a memo written to the Robertson panel and the organizers, which were the Air Force and the CIA. That was my first shock, that the Air Force was there as a contractor to the intelligence community. That's really understandable, but it was at a much higher level in terms of the global and scientific access to data than just what the Air Force was supposed to be doing.

The second surprise I had was that those two pages were still marked secret in red and the term "secret" had not been scratched out and revised. This was 1968, so that kind of document should have expired as a secret document, but it wasn't. I had a problem of what to do with it. I consulted Dr.

Hynek who was the only person I took into my confidence. We decided to approach an organization that could declassify it.

The first thing I did was to hire an attorney, familiar with the government, to find out the procedure for declassification of documents. We wrote to the Air Force because the document was partly an Air Force file. The Air Force sent us a mimeographed circular that said, "If you're interested in Blue Book, you can ask for the microfilm. This is how you do it. It's deposited at such and such a depository," and that was the end of it. They never really responded to our request.

At the time, I was working with a Senate panel regarding access to computer networks. I had met a very highly placed attorney, who was in charge on the Senate side of handling data from the military. I explained the situation to him. He said, "Send me the original memo through secure mail, and I will see that it's declassified." I went through the legislative branch because I knew that if we submitted it to the Pentagon it would disappear, which we didn't want. This attorney happened to be the general counsel for the congressional committee that supervised the Pentagon's budget and he could technically turn off their budget. So, he was in a good situation to declassify that memo, and he made the memo available.

Suddenly, people became aware that there was much more behind the Robertson panel than what the public had been told: that, in fact, they had done a very, very thorough job of reviewing the information. But the question was, what was that memo doing there? The memo came from the contractor, Battelle Memorial Institute, which was responsible, initially, for the files that went to Blue Book. They had just done an official review of the Blue Book files with a large budget for the time—a budget that was comparatively bigger than that of the Condon committee.

The memo recommended that the Robertson panel not be called, because there were missing areas of research that would complete the information. It was premature to gather these top five scientists—including a Nobel Prize-winning physicist—to review incomplete data. It was a very thoughtful, very smart memo addressed to the real organizers of the panel: the CIA. It was ignored. The panel went on.

The rest of it is still classified. I hope there are still a few people who remember what happened, because I'd really like to know if what Battelle recommended was ever implemented. They had a number of recommendations on what UFO research should be done. There are many areas of darkness that, from a historical perspective, are extremely interesting. I hope that the initiative by Congress is going to bring that to the light of day.

Mishlove: I think one of the areas that must have been of concern even as early as 1954, and is probably still of great concern today, is the seeming relationship between UFO sightings and various nuclear facilities, particularly those in the United States.

Vallée: One of the better databases was developed by the French government, and it's now public but the public doesn't know that it's public. It's a very, very good database including aircraft pilot sightings and has about 3,000 cases. The database we were working from had about 800 cases. Dr. Richard Haines from NASA and I collaborated in building the database, but the main developer worked for the French government executive branch, primarily in defense.

They looked at military cases, civilian cases, and private aircraft sightings with the pilots themselves being interviewed on the record. They've recorded radar visual data from military pilots, private pilots, and airline pilots. The data is extremely rich and we've been analyzing it. There is a discrimination factor in the database between the military planes being approached by UFOs and the civilian planes reporting UFOs.

I don't think anybody in the US has picked up on that research, but it's certainly something that should be done. It's one of the databases that we turned over to Bigelow Aerospace, to the AATIP (Advanced Aerospace Threat Identification Program), but I don't think it has been analyzed. I'm no longer privy to what has happened to the databases that we created because the project was classified. I had top-secret clearance, like the rest of the team in Las Vegas, working with the Bigelow Aerospace Project. That particular part of the database is not classified. It's open, which has been integrated within the 260,000 cases worldwide.

What that study revealed was a radical difference between the behavior of the phenomenon when it was approaching a military aircraft and a civilian aircraft. That needs to be reinvestigated with more data because the database is twenty years old. If that's verified, it means that the phenomenon has a special interest in military craft and facilities, and it displays a different behavior in the other ninety percent of the civilian cases when it's being seen over fields, cities, and other areas.

Mishlove: How would you characterize that radical difference?

Vallée: If you remember the Steven Spielberg movie *Close Encounters of the Third Kind* where the control tower says, "Do you want to report a UFO?" There is a long silence. One of the pilots finally says, "Negative, we don't want to report." The radar shows civilian airliners being approached by UFOs. Many of the real cases were, in fact, reported and we have the transcripts from the pilots.

An object, a light, or sometimes a well-defined object comes and paces or goes around the aircraft and is seen by pilots, passengers and radar. Then it will go away. There are cases where several radar stations throughout a city tracked both the UFO and the aircraft. Everybody knows that. Of course, it was denied for many years because the airlines didn't want any trouble; nor did they want people to be scared. Dr. Haines, with his organization, has done a great job of contributing to that civilian database. That's available if people wanted to take the trouble to look.

The military cases are very different. Typically, when an object arrives. It's perceived as a threat by the aircraft and the devices on the aircraft will pick it up. First the radar, then infrared sensors, and then other sensors, some of which may be classified, will interrogate and gather data about the object. That's not the end of it. The object seems to be completely aware that it's being watched and may not only pace the aircraft, it may also go around it. It can even place itself into a collision course. There was a case described before the United Nations in 1978, by one of the pilots of an army helicopter that was on a collision course with an object that came straight at their helicopter. The helicopter went into a crash maneuver, essentially, going down as fast as a helicopter could. It was one of the UH-1H helicopters with four military members on board, and they experienced that.

Here you have a maneuver, which has to be interpreted as a hostile. I asked the helicopter pilot, Captain Coyne, privately, when we were at the United Nations, "What went through your mind when you could not avoid the collision?" He said, "Sir, I closed my eyes and prepared to die." That's a military officer that's not afraid of saying that he had exhausted all the maneuvers to avoid the collision. It turned out, the object came rushing at the helicopter and then stopped above it. It was not the little helicopter you see over San Francisco or Albuquerque—it raised the helicopter two thousand feet in a few seconds. All the controls were down for a crash landing, but the helicopter was still going up.

Captain Coyne, as part of our panel, described that event before the full political committee of the United Nations and the entire room was completely silent. When he said, "I closed my eyes and prepared to die," as an Army military officer, that was a very special moment.

That characterizes that there is direct intention of the phenomenon to prove something. Under those circumstances, it had to be interpreted as hostile. But, frankly, there was nothing they could do. They couldn't shoot at it, or do anything else. Nobody would come to help them. Fortunately, the helicopter was released and the object went off. There is no way to avoid looking at this as an attempt to make itself known. This is not something you can keep on denying, no matter how many PhDs you have. I hear people on the radio saying, "Well, it was just a balloon," come on. Or, "They didn't see very well." That team was coming back to their base in Ohio from an eye exam because the Army mandates that you have to have good vision to fly helicopters, which is a reasonable thing to do. So, when the skeptics say, "Well, you know, they had fuzzy vision; they were tired," and so on, that's just complete ignorance—complete negligence, actually.

That's the difference between the behavior of the phenomenon when it's over a base, a nuclear facility, or near a military aircraft, than near commercial, or private aircraft. Those are the things that people need to know if they are going to restart the research in a serious way. They need to look at the work that has been done over the last fifty years, going through these phases and accumulating the data. The people who documented this were not a bunch of stupid people in Silicon Valley—as I've been told recently—or a bunch of amateurs, although the amateurs have done a good job. They were teams of professional scientists from different disciplines, looking at this with military officers and pilots, and retired commercial pilots on unpaid time, documenting the data.

Fortunately, the computing technology that we have now is way above what would have been in a university computing center twenty years ago. Don't say that this was amateur research that we can now forget, and now we're going to do it right. We need everybody involved; we need all the data; we need to look at what has been done in the past.

Mishlove: I seem to recall there have been reports of UFOs appearing in the vicinity of nuclear missile sites, I think maybe in North Dakota for example, and disarming the missile relaunch/launch mechanisms. I don't know whether that's true, but I would think that sort of thing would be of great interest today to the military.

Vallée: That is true, and it has been true in several countries. There have been meetings that are on the record between the US and, first, with the Soviet Union, and more recently with Russia, because the Russians had the same experience. There may be a nuclear exchange at some point due to the war between Russia and Ukraine and nobody wants to launch an intercontinental nuclear missile by mistake. It was thought that there were guidelines to prevent missiles going off unintentionally. Some of those launch incidents got the attention of the security people worldwide, because if somebody can take control of a nuclear launch site, then a lot of precautions have to be reconsidered, and of course that's beyond my level. It's beyond the level of the people in Congress. It has to be done at an international level where we can discuss it realistically with our potential enemies. That's a very different kind of meeting.

Mishlove: I'm under the impression that in the popular UFO culture, which is something of a circus, there is a belief that these UFOs will save us from ourselves if it ever came to nuclear war, and that's what they're demonstrating.

Vallée: I followed that for a while. It would be nice to entertain that idea. The fact is that we came very, very close to nuclear war. That near miss has happened in several countries. In the US it has happened three times, including one time when the system was at a high DEFCON classification, the B-52s had taken off, and had to be recalled. There were no UFOs intervening to stop it. It's a nice idea, but I don't think that they care that much about it.

Mishlove: In terms of the present era and what we can look forward to is—will the United States develop a government-sponsored, non-military research program of the sort you mentioned has been going on in France for the last forty years?

Vallée: That's really one of the questions facing both Congress and the Pentagon today. Some people have already responded on the record at Congressional hearings. I heard one of the officers say that this should be looked at solely within the United States, because of the potential of enemies discovering strategically important information. The defense industry could learn something from looking at the US for records, which they've been doing, but with much greater resources across the military branches so that the US could have better defense technologies. That's a valid idea. It's certainly one that will be at the forefront before Congress. Congress will have to make a decision on this based on the assessment of the analysts. That's what the analysts are for on both sides of the fence.

This is potentially a threat to humanity. If you take these descriptions seriously—and now you have to take them seriously—because, looking at the data that has been vetted, we have all the parameters. We can answer pretty much any question that the academy could have. People are going to discover, if the current effort goes on—which I hope to live long enough to see—that objects have been recovered and that we have access to the materials. We've already done research at our own level to document that, both in my books in *Trinity*, and also in the lab. We've published the results in the scientific press, so this is on the record. It's not a rumor. It's not just a bunch of nice people with ideas. We can build on what we know with other countries. That's what that meeting in France was all about.

One of the questions that people ask me is, since I'm in the fairly unique position of having access to the US data since I was part of AATIP and other projects. I'm also on the advisory board for the French CNES for the last five years. I know the French government data and I know the French government channels that are used to filter, examine, and access the data. So, people say, "Why don't the other countries come up with their data and publish it?" The French have published their data. It's on the record, it's on the Internet, anybody can look at it. They have not been completely open with the rest of it at the government level and the French government has never said, "We think there are UFOs."

They encourage research on any unknown subject in science. A lot of cancer research involves the unknown. The shape of the universe is unknown. What genetically determines the date of the birth of a baby is unknown. There are a number of open subjects in science, and UFOs are one of them. The French government has never said, "We believe that there are real UFOs, and that the United States should communicate with us."

The reason is—and it's a puzzle for many people that I know in Silicon Valley—the French have all this data; why don't they go public and say, "We're going to study it openly because we believe that the phenomenon is real." They haven't taken that step because everybody is in awe of the power, and frankly, the resources and astronomers of the United States and the Academy of Sciences. American science is number one, not in every area, but it's number one in most important areas of science. No scientist in France wants to volunteer to go against that with a proclamation that UFOs are real and potentially an important scientific endeavor, because of potential ridicule by the American Academy of Sciences.

The American Academy of Sciences has never reversed its assessment that there is nothing to UFO phenomena, even now. We know members of the Academy were open to, encouraging, and participating in research through the Academy of Medicine, or the Academy of Technology, or the Academy of Science. But there's no public statement from the Academy. Until that happens, I doubt that any academician or any top scientist with a lab and a good budget, is going to go public that UFO phenomena are real until the US does it first.

Mishlove: So in other words, we're really not yet in a new era, we're maybe on the cusp. Certainly, the *New York Times* has gone public, but that's really not enough.

Vallée: The last time the *New York Times* went public about UFOs was *when* they published the Condon Report. They said that nobody should study UFOs because it was a waste of money and there was nothing there. *The New York Times* has a business to run.

Mishlove: They have released the Navy photos of the sightings off the coast of California. That's well acknowledged at this point. I think the report that went to Congress seemed like an official government acknowledgement that there is unknown phenomena. Now they're calling it unidentified aerial phenomena [UAP] rather than UFOs, maybe as a way to separate themselves from the earlier world. But, I still hear you saying that they haven't gone far enough yet.

Vallée: We're not there yet. I think the breakthrough has come from a small number of very courageous people going public, including officers from the Pentagon. Those with the right credentials, including Mr. Christopher Mellon who was a former US Deputy Assistant Secretary of Defense for Intelligence under two presidents, can call attention to the data and then push for data to be released. The Nimitz photographs and infrared films are a part of that and at least two other cases. There are other cases that are still classified that were also shown to Congress.

I'm happy to have lived long enough to see that sea change where the phenomenon has been acknowledged officially. The scientific community has looked at that and many members of the scientific community have gone public and even created their own organizations to say: "Now we're ready to study this with the resources at our disposal, with our labs, with our computers, with our microscopes."

A number of scientists I've worked with, including Dr. Garry Nolan at Stanford, have started to put their lab facilities to work on some of the data. I've transferred to Dr. Nolan my entire collection of residual materials from a number of cases, and we are studying them together. There is a small team now in California and a small team at Harvard under Dr. Avi Loeb developing new optical systems to document what's going on. There are at least two major universities where first-rate scientists are at work, on their own time, with their own budgets, developing these new methodologies and new instruments.

That's *not* American science dedicating itself, or part of itself, to a major study.

I've seen this three times in my now long life. I've seen it first with the moon shot. I can remember sitting in my living room back in New Jersey, in the 1960s with my two little kids and my wife, watching somebody walk on the moon, on TV, at prime time. Everybody around the world was watching. There were eleven manned missions to the moon by the United States. Then for the next fifty years, nothing happened.

Nothing happened because Congress said, "We're not ready; the technology is not ready," which is probably true. But NASA could have developed better technology back then. Until SpaceX, we didn't have a rocket that could go back to the moon. SpaceX is only about twenty percent more powerful than the Saturn V that we had in the early 1970s. Twenty percent in fifty years doesn't do it. It's a failure of technology.

We're going to go back to the moon better prepared with better medical support, better training, better everything so it will be safer. However, we've lost a rocket recently; we know the technology is not one-hundred percent reliable yet.

A second example is the Internet. Paul Baran, who invented the ARPANET, is not well known though he worked at the RAND Corporation, a research and development branch of the US Air Force. He had the vision of a network where you could have packets that could go everywhere and was essentially indestructible. He did it both for commercial reasons, which people still don't understand today, and for military reasons. Nobody paid attention. It took him four years to get the Pentagon to dedicate a small amount of money to build the ARPANET, which was an experimental Internet.

He is the real grandfather of everything we use today, which was packet technology. When the French put together a national network, they ignored the packet technology completely and it didn't survive. The Internet just took over worldwide because it was based on packet switching. Paul Baran was my mentor in computer science. I then became one of the principal investigators for ARPA at the Department of Defense. We built the first computer conferences on the network and turned it into a commercial facility. Good software gets forgotten, because good software plunges in the depth of a machine and people don't see it. If it's really good software, people shouldn't know it's there. It should be reliable. You shouldn't have to mess with it. That's the kind of software we built.

Then the ARPANET died, just like the Moon project. The Pentagon said, "Well, we've proved it. We can use it. We don't need to continue paying for it." It was picked up by the National Science Foundation, which is a public unclassified science agency funded by the US government, a major funding agency for science. The NSF picked it up because it saved money by linking together different universities that were doing the same research. Why buy computers for every one of them, when you could network all the computers together? It was pure genius that this was the engine that could revolutionize American science. They did it without telling anybody. They just started funding a number of facilities around the country.

It was a mistake at the beginning, because there were many different Internets until they got the idea: "We need to have just one massive Internet." The public only became aware of it about 1996, 1997, when the web was invented in Switzerland by a very, very bright young computer scientist, who just hacked together the piece of software that everybody could use. Everybody loved it the first day, and that became the web. But it wasn't done with American dollars.

That's the history of the Internet that the people using the web today have no idea about. I had the privilege of living through that but there was a period of fifty years when nothing happened. We're doing the same thing with UFOs today. There was good research on UFOs fifty years ago like the research that Battelle was doing in 1954. The next high water mark is what Bob Bigelow and our team did that resulted in AATIP. That became public because of Mr. Mellon, and Mr. Luis Elizondo, bringing it before Congress, reviving the idea and showing how it could be done. The project itself died and all the work that we'd done died with it. Somebody will revive it again, just like the moon shot has been revived by Elon Musk, not by NASA. For some reason, even in this area of high technology, things have to die for fifty years before the public can really benefit from it.

Mishlove: Given that history, it makes me think about the field of parapsychology. I know you've been somewhat aligned with that field as well. I got my doctoral degree in 1980. Throughout the 1970s, there seemed to be a period in which we all expected enormous progress. The work in remote viewing was very promising. Yet, while the Internet has achieved its full potential, or close to it, parapsychology has yet to do so, like the field of UFO research.

Vallée: We demonstrated that the Internet was the ideal technological tool to conduct sophisticated scientific remote viewing experiments, which has never been exploited to the scale where it could be. It's a free resource. You don't need to write a grant application to use the Internet. It's one more revolution that should be coming.

Mishlove: It's been a real pleasure to have this conversation with you and to have a sense of where we stand today in these important areas of research. Many people would say nothing could be more important than understanding the mystery that UFOs represent. I tend to think the mystery of parapsychology is probably equally important and probably related. I want to thank you so much for spending this time with me. I'm hopeful that we can have many more conversations.

Vallée: It would be my pleasure. Thank you very much.

2

High Strangeness, UFOs, and the Afterlife
with
Nick Cook

Jeffrey Mishlove: Hello and welcome. I'm Jeffrey Mishlove. Our topic today is "High Strangeness, UFOs and the Afterlife." My guest is Nick Cook, who is the author of twenty fiction and nonfiction titles, including *The Hunt for Zero Point: Inside the Classified World of Anti-Gravity Technology*, as well as a popular parapsychological thriller, *The Grid*. He is the former aviation editor of *Jane's Defence Weekly*. This interview was recorded in a hotel room in Las Vegas where the two of us were attending the Bigelow Institute of Consciousness Studies award ceremony for their essay competition.

Welcome, Nick. Why don't we start with the story of your grandmother's death?

Nick Cook: My parents divorced when I was five. My sister and I moved in with my grandparents, in a large rambling country house in the southeast of England. About a year and a half into living with my grandparents, my grandmother sadly died. She was American, so she did the reverse thing. She came over to

England and married my grandfather. Quite a stiff upper lip family, not used to discussing feelings, but my grandmother was a very passionate—as you'd expect from my American cousins—passionate and sort of hot-blooded. She was also interested in the paranormal. Maybe a couple of days after she died, my father came back to console my grandfather at the house.

There had been some rather strange goings on since my grandmother had died. She used to go up to the attic when she couldn't sleep, because she was an insomniac, and she would sweep out the attic. When she'd been alive, you could hear the clack, clack, clack of her broom working against pieces of furniture and the sideboard in the attic. My father was awoken by this one night after my grandmother died, to hear this going on, but that wasn't the strangest thing. The strangest thing was he and my grandfather were having a discussion about my grandmother's will, and they disagreed on a point. At that moment, there was a lamp between them: a heavy Victorian lamp that lifted up, did a bit of a tilt and a wobble, and then plonked very loudly back down on the table between them again.

I was only six or seven or something when this happened, so I didn't know anything about it at the time. But my father, who was an engineer and quite a rational person, told the family—this sort of got handed down in family lore afterwards—including to my sister and me. It's when you get testimony like that from someone you know and trust—as I obviously did with my dad, who was intensely curious about this incident—that you can believe what they're saying. He was obviously very upset at the time that his mother had died, but he always wanted to know how that lamp picked up in the way that it did; how energy had been transferred from somewhere to that lamp. The whole consciousness aspect of it, he put to one side. But that was really one of those inciting (*sic*) moments in my life when I thought, "Well, there's got to be an awful lot more to our existence than is merely set out by our 3D, four-dimensional physics". So, that was the story of my grandfather, my grandmother, and the lamp.

Mishlove: There were other events in your family as well.

Cook: Definitely there were. My mother-in-law died in 2014. There were maybe seven or eight of us from her extended family who attended her while she was dying, including my wife who was holding her mom's hand. At the precise moment that my mother-in-law died, my wife, instead of being extremely upset and distressed at this moment, as anyone would be, she stood up and announced to everyone in the room that all is well. Everyone was shocked, and I was stunned. I thought, "Why are you saying this? It's your mom, your dear beloved mom has just this second passed away, and yet you're telling the room that all is well."

Maybe an hour or two later when we were sitting down, I asked my wife about this. I said, "Why did you say that?" She said to me, "Weren't you there as well?" I said, "Where?" She said, "In that space where time stopped, but it stretched infinitely. I was connected to everything. I knew everything. This place was more real than real, and it was imbued with a feeling that I can only describe as all-encompassing, joyous love." I thought, "What is this thing that she's describing?" I came from a very nuts and bolts background. I'm a technology journalist, but I'm a curious person, and I wanted to know how this person, whom I trusted intimately—we'd been married at that point, maybe 25 years—I wanted to know what she was talking about.

When I googled this thing, I realized that what she was describing was something called a shared death experience. That was the primary exciting thing that made me want to go and research consciousness, because I had to rationalize what my wife had discovered. In a sense, that linked back to what my dad had told me about my grandmother and the lamp. Those two things combined really set me off on this journey.

Mishlove: I gather that at the same time you were beginning to explore consciousness, you had already had some exposure to the UFO field.

Cook: For some fifteen-odd years, I had been the aerospace editor of a publication called *Jane's Defence Weekly*, which is a military affairs journal. It's bought by professionals in defense and intelligence communities. It's a really serious publication, and I enjoyed writing for it immensely because it got me all over the world. I was able to meet some very interesting people and to pursue my curiosity about interesting technology, but secret things, too.

During the early years at the magazine, I was particularly involved in uncovering stories about very secret defense projects—particularly in aerospace—that were going on in the U.S. where most, if not all, of the really cutting-edge and interesting technology was to be had. Some of this technology, particularly to do with stealth, was highly secret, but also so shrouded in secrecy that some of the things that people said they saw in the skies, particularly in the desert southwest, were often mistaken for UFOs. In that sense, my nuts and bolts rationalist job in this very serious publication started to cross over into the UFO domain. I was very keen to separate out the stuff that you could explain by technology, science, and engineering with the stuff that couldn't be explained.

I wrote a book about this called *The Hunt for Zero Point*, which was my attempt to segregate out that which could be explained by exotic technology, and that might, I speculated, be to do with breakthroughs in propulsion physics. Perhaps there are some new esoteric forms of energy and propulsion which would look an awful lot like a UFO, if you were to build one here on Earth. I think I did that, at least to my curiosity and satisfaction. I was able to look at terrestrial technology and ask the question, "Are what people commonly say are UFOs are' any of that stuff built here on Earth in great secrecy?" I think, unquestionably, some of it could have been.

To my mind, there was a significant proportion of sightings that could not be explained by anything that I would remotely describe as "rational." That always left me intrigued. I had to professionally put it to one side until the US Navy article came out in the *New York Times*. They had a big story in 2017 about how the US Navy had been encountering a plethora of UFOs off both the west coast and the east coast of the U.S., amongst its carrier battle groups. These sightings were so well documented and so strange that it emboldened me to say, "Look, this stuff really needs to be acknowledged and talked about now." I felt confident enough post-2017 to really get my teeth into the subject in a way that I had not before.

Mishlove: Based on your essay in the Bigelow Institute competition, you see a relationship between survival after death and these mysterious UFO sightings and a wide spectrum of other phenomena?

Cook: I spent a long time looking at exotic nuts and bolts technology, and metaphorically giving that a really good kick in the tires of it. I realized that I could explain the stuff that had been built on Earth unquestionably. But that other category of sightings, which defied a rational explanation, needed another approach, in my opinion. It couldn't be explained or analyzed critically by looking at it from a nuts and bolts perspective.

Mishlove: You're referring to the reports of the Navy that were released in 2017? You don't believe that there's a mechanical explanation for those sightings?

Cook: Well, I'm jumping ahead a little bit here, because I think they are both. I think the UFO phenomenon, in a sense, gets to the heart of my essay. What I'm talking about in the essay is what I call an interface, where our consciousness interacts with a wider consciousness. In this interface, a lot of interesting, unexplained stuff happens. I think that the survival of our consciousness, post-material death, manifests on this interface. But I think a range of other phenomena do as well. For instance the near-death experience, out-of-body experience, and remote viewing.

In terms of the UFO phenomenon, I think that also resides somewhere on this interface, in that, at times, it takes on a physical aspect. When it takes on that attribute, you could—again, metaphorically—pick up a brick, throw it against that UFO, and that brick is going to go clang because in that moment that UFO is real. But there is another aspect to the UFO phenomenon, which is more metaphysical and has, as others have documented, psychic qualities to it. There is so much high strangeness around the phenomenon when it is in that state, that it takes on this non-physical attribute.

So many people have tried to analyze the UFO phenomenon from the nuts and bolts side. I thought the only way that I felt I could make any headway myself was to come at it from the other direction, which was from this metaphysical consciousness-related aspect. There are the phenomena alongside the UFO itself: to wit poltergeist phenomena, instances of psychokinesis, telepathy, even, strange as it may sound, the appearance of cryptozoological creatures. All of that seems to reside on this spectrum. So that's the direction that I wanted to take a look at it from.

Mishlove: Out of the blue, at some point, you received a grant from a billionaire to begin to explore this area.

Cook: Yeah, it's extraordinary the way these things work because, after my wife's shared death experience with her mom, I wanted to get my teeth into the whole consciousness field, but it wasn't my field. Professionally I had no excuse at all to investigate it. We've all got to put bread on the table, and my profession lay elsewhere.

In addition to being a nonfiction writer, I occasionally dip into the world of fiction and write thrillers. Having done a bit of background research on this shared death phenomenon between my wife and her mom, I put that research into this thriller, a book that came out in 2019 called *The Grid*. I became so intrigued by it that I wanted to continue that research, but I had no means legitimately to pursue it professionally. I expressed this ambition through a sort of aphorism or mantra that I wrote on my wall at the beginning of 2019 as a goal for the next year, which said, "I would like to work with the world's leading researchers in the consciousness field," and left it at that.

I had no means by which to accomplish this or achieve this goal because it was so outside the field that I had been working in up to that point. But then, lo and behold, I get this grant from a philanthropic individual whom I met, and he said, "I would like to help." We'd never discussed what my interests were, but somehow he intuited that I was interested in the consciousness field and wanted to put some money towards helping my research. That's what happened. I got this grant from him to pursue the subject of consciousness for the next two years, which ultimately gave me the research material that I put into the BICS essay.

Mishlove: I know, for example, along the way you met my good friend Gail Hayssen, who has been a guest on this channel several times. She's a remarkable individual who recommended to me that we should get together. She thought the world of you.

Cook: I think the world of Gail. She, as you know, is a shaman. Again, shamanism was something way outside my knowledge base. When I was researching the consciousness field, I was particularly interested in approaching it from an omnidirectional aspect. I wanted to get in touch with experiencers in multidisciplinary realms. Remote viewers, near-death experiencers, out-of-body experiencers, shamans, channelers—the plethora. Through talking to each of them, I wanted to see whether there were any shared characteristics of their experience that might inform the consciousness field as a whole.

I had no idea how to approach a shaman. I didn't know any. We don't have too many who live around us in southwest London. I approached Dean Radin, because we have a mutual friend, and he put me in touch with a range of experiencers, including Gail Hayssen. Because it came through Dean, whose reputation in this field is stellar, I knew that in a sense, he'd already done the due diligence on these people. I didn't need to check them out to know whether they were reliable. Gail was able to tell me remarkable things about how she works and her own experiences of shamanism, thanks to Dean.

Mishlove: You found some common elements in these diverse areas. Some people might think that shamanism, for example, is completely separate from UFOs.

Cook: To my satisfaction, I was able to find a good many common elements between these experiencers, who include amongst them, of course, those who have experimented with psychedelics—LSD, DMT, or whatever. What I found was too striking. This was a non-scientific survey because I didn't gather the data with the rigor that would be approved of for an empirical study, but it passed muster for me. There were a number of commonalities amongst all of these experiencers, which led to two things that stood out when I cross-referenced the data. One was encounters with entities. There were spirit-like beings, entities—call them what you will—that all of these experiencers said they encountered when they were in a state, whatever that state was, or however they came to be in that state.

In Gail's case, it was a shamanistic encounter, but in Eben Alexander's, it was a near-death experience. That was one interesting point for me. They had this common point of reference of encounters with beings who they felt to be consciousnesses in their own right, in that they had their own individuality about them and their own individual mode of expression.

The second was an encounter with what they felt came under a different range of names: the source, the creator, the absolute, a point of infinite vibration and light that I suppose some might call God. Those were the two really interesting points that stood out in this omnidirectional sort of survey that I'd done. It told me something deeply numinous about the quality of consciousness, but which again allowed me to believe that this is a subject that can and should be explored by mainstream science in a way that mainstream science has not to this point. But I see signs that it is increasingly engaging in the study of consciousness and a recognition, perhaps, that consciousness is primary, and matter secondary. We're not there yet, obviously, but I feel that there are encouraging signs that the flip may be on its way.

Mishlove: Let's go back to the UFO sightings reported by the military. Did you, in probing those experiences, discover numinous qualities there?

Cook: A report was commissioned on UFOs by the United States Congress and appeared in June 2021 on the phenomenon. This was delivered by the defense and intelligence community to Congress as a sort of, "Here's what we know about UFOs," or UAP to give them their kosher acronym, Unidentified Aerial Phenomena. Many people were disappointed by this report because they said it didn't go far enough to explain what the US defense and intelligence communities knew about UFOs. I happen to think it was a real breakthrough because it was a real acknowledgement that there is a phenomenon here that needs to be taken seriously.

Among the data in a very slimmed down—I think it's a seven page unclassified version of the report is a small section of sightings that totally defies explanation. That is the portion that everyone is interested in. It's not the bit that you can analyze and dismiss as top-secret technology that may have been developed by foreign militaries. With that subset, there is no doubt that there is a range of strange phenomena that accompany the UFO itself.

The researcher Jacques Vallée, whose work is exemplary, details the strangeness of that phenomenon, something in fact he dubbed "high strangeness." Because that phenomenon is so off-putting to intelligence and defense communities who just want to come up with an answer to the technology of UFOs as a potential threat, they have dismissed it, and they've only analyzed the UFO as a nuts and bolts phenomenon. I think that's wrong. As Jacques Vallée and others have documented, unfortunately for those who want to analyze this rationally and critically, it is accompanied by this stuff that defies an explanation.

Mishlove: Can you give an example of high strangeness?

Cook: I'm trying to think of a specific UFO case example. There are so many of them.

Mishlove: One that was included in the government report?

Cook: The government report in the unclassified version was so watered down that all it talked about was a handful of sightings that it had looked at since 2004. As anyone who's ever done any research in the field knows, the UFO phenomenon goes way back. Certainly in the modern era, it's been charted since 1947 when Kenneth Arnold first cited what he described as flying objects that looked like saucers skipping over the surface of a pond, which gave rise to the description flying saucer.

Since that era, there have been so many sightings, but in the report that was given to Congress, the intelligence community and the defense community said, "We're only going to look back to 2004 and analyze data since 2004," suggesting that that was the only data that was worth looking at. But actually, what that managed to do was [to] obscure the long trail of historical sightings going back to 1947, in which there is so much good data, including some pretty scary stuff, ostensibly, about how UFOs have consistently interfered with the nuclear deterrent, which is extremely well documented and has been for a very long time. I suspect, probably, that is why it has been left out because the U.S. military does not want to acknowledge that there are things in the sky, which defy rational explanation.

Mishlove: It seems that nuts and bolts machines, let's say, that come from another world somewhere, might well be interested in our nuclear developments here.

Cook: Indeed. I think that is part of this all, in that that is one way of looking at it. If you are charged with analysis of something that is appearing in your sky which you can't explain, you have to consider, if this is your job, that it may be a threat. On the other hand, it might not be. If it is truly esoteric in nature, it may be bound up in all sorts of other things.

Going back to that discussion we were having earlier about this perceptual interface. If I am perceiving things in a space that is governed by an aspect of consciousness that is not well understood, it is entirely possible that these things, whether they are ghosts or UFOs, are appearing on this interface as some manifestation of perhaps, Jung's collective unconscious. Jung himself was very interested in the UFO phenomenon and felt that it was both precognitive and reflective in some way, perhaps some aspect of our group mind that is reflected in the way that we perceive things. So, yes, there is a nuts and bolts aspect to it, but at the same time, that doesn't explain every aspect of it either.

Mishlove: Speaking personally, I have lots of data that I think would link UFO phenomena to life after death, but I'm just curious as to what data might have been revealed by the US government along these lines.

Cook: I don't think the US government has revealed any data that connects the UFO phenomenon to other aspects of paranormality or consciousness precisely for that reason. I think it is because the government is, along with everyone else, struggling to make those kinds of connections. Were it to make those connections, I think that in their minds there would be ridicule attached to it because you're starting to veer away from the defense aspect of it, which is nuts and bolts, into this esoteric realm wherein you make yourself open to criticism that you've "lost the plot." You're veering into the subject that is more commonly explored by religion or philosophy, and that's not the role of defense or the intelligence community, they would say. I think that is why, too, a lack of progress has been made in the analysis and examination by "defense-type people" of this phenomenon is because they're looking at it through a very narrow aperture.

Mishlove: Do you think they are hiding information?

Cook: Inevitably, if a government is analyzing something that it doesn't understand, it is going to hide that because it doesn't want to display its own ignorance. That exposes a vulnerability in a nation's security, or in anyone's security. That's a very uncomfortable place to be in if you are charged with national security. Yes, there is a great deal of secrecy surrounding the subject, but I don't think it's all to do with what many people believe, which is that it's because the government is hiding away crashed extraterrestrial craft or because it's got aliens in freezers. I think a lot of it is just to hide its own ignorance, actually.

Mishlove: I don't know if you're familiar with a book I wrote over twenty years ago around the same time you were working on *The Hunt for Zero Point Energy*, which undoubtedly takes you back to Hal Puthoff's research. I met Hal Puthoff myself in 1976, and he dumped a big file into my lap. He said, "Please take it off of my hands. We don't want it here at SRI. It's too controversial." A man who called himself the PK Man could produce UFO sightings at will and did so.

Cook: Who was the PK Man?

Mishlove: His name was Ted Owens.

Cook: No, I don't know about him. I will get the name of your book afterwards because I'd love to read it. I do know Hal Puthoff. I've met him quite a few times and we've talked predominantly about the zero point energy aspect of his research. We've spoken less about the remote viewing side of his career. But in all the realms that he's been involved in, yes, there are some very interesting things. I would love to read your book.

Mishlove: If I may, let me share with you one story because I think it is on point. It is the example that you would need to make this connection clear. In 1976, when I first met Ted Owens,

I was a graduate student and just beginning my explorations in parapsychology. He had a high stack of papers of demonstrations he had produced. I noticed several instances in which he said, "I'm going to produce a UFO, and you will see it within a certain time and space parameters," and that happened. They were reported in newspapers, and so I asked him, "Can you do that for me?" I had all of Hal Puthoff's files at that point. He was so glad to get it out of his office.

Ted Owens said, "Yes, I can create three UFO sightings that will occur within a 90-day window within 100 miles of San Francisco." At one point he called me up in the middle of this experiment. He was very excited, and he said, "Jeffrey, I can feel it coming. This is going to be big. This is going to be a sighting that will be seen by hundreds of people. It will be photographed and a picture will be published on the front page of one of your local newspapers." Three days later that is exactly what happened.

Cook: Wow. I would love to see that. I'm particularly interested since Hal handed that data off to you. So what you are saying, Jeff, is an example of a crossover between the UFO phenomenon and mind. How we are able to either project it or reflect it. I agree that there is that crossover. It's taken on a new form now in something which I'm sure you're aware of called CE5, close encounters of the fifth kind, wherein experiencers invite contact with the phenomenon. I'm not altogether sure it's a good idea, by the way, in all cases. But that's what they do. This often elicits encounters with orbs and UFO-like phenomena.

It is very well documented that it's not often solo experiencers who are calling these things down, but they are witnessed by multiple people—that that is the crossover. That is another example of how these two apparently separate fields interact. That's the space that I want to look at next.

Mishlove: I'll give you another example. It relates even more directly to the question of survival. Ted Owens was a very interesting man. I've written a book about him called *The PK*

Man. It hasn't sold a lot of copies yet, but I do keep talking about it.

Cook: You're going to get one more sale now. [Laughter]

Mishlove: He died in 1987. He was living in a farmhouse at the time in Fort Ann, New York, a tiny little town. He said that he had received messages from the UFOs to rendezvous with him there. He produced, in my research with him, 168 demonstrations of psychokinetic phenomena that he claimed were mediated by his contact with—he called them the space intelligences—hyperspace entities who hovered above the earth in an invisible UFO. He claimed that they had directed him to Fort Ann. That's where he died, incidentally, of sclerosis of the liver. He drank a lot. In fact, he was a very heavy drinker. He seemed to produce a lot of psychokinetic phenomena while inebriated. But before he died, he sent me a number of newspaper clippings showing UFOs appearing around Fort Ann and also a letter of testimony from his neighbor who claimed that UFOs were hovering right above his farmhouse. He died shortly thereafter.

Cook: Time and again, you hear this kind of story, and it becomes important. It certainly has become important to me when I hear from sources that I trust. We talked at the beginning about getting information from sources that you trust when you're exploring this subject. In my case, it was from my father and from my wife. In my work as a senior editor at *Jane's Defence Weekly*, I was introduced to not only Hal Puthoff, but Ingo Swann who were the godfathers or fathers of remote viewing. I had several chances to talk to them about their work, which was funded by the government for a long time. As a defense journalist, I looked for patterns. In fact, I adhered to the Woodward and Bernstein mantra of following the money. When there's 15 plus years of constant funding by the defense and intelligence community into a thing—in this case, remote viewing—that's when I sit up and take notice.

Uri Geller, whom I've also met, invited me to his home after he'd read *The Hunt for Zero Point,* and he did the spoon-bending thing for me. Uri was also funded by the CIA and when Hal was at SRI, Stanford Research Institute, he analyzed Uri's work. All of these things have a very solid base to them for me. But that's the foundational stuff. I think if we're going to make progress going forward, we need to look—I think it's probably Hal Puthoff who describes it as "the frontier of the frontier." That will entail exploring aspects of consciousness, which will be deeply uncomfortable for some areas of science, because it will exhibit high strangeness of the kind talked about by Jacques Vallée.

Mishlove: It seems as if, at least since maybe the early 1950s, there was an official policy in the government to try and debunk these high strangeness reports in order to avoid public panic.

Cook: Definitely. That has been a part of my work as well. From the defense journalism realm you become acutely aware that not all the information that you get is necessarily the truth or correct. You have to employ a very rigorous filter to try and work out what is truth and what isn't, particularly with aspects of national security. Yes, the whole UFO field has been riven with disinformation, as is well documented in the 1950s and 1960s when the CIA, among others, were behind a range of new technology that was appearing in the skies, such as the U-2 spy plane and the very fast flying A-12 hypersonic aircraft. They were aware that the UFO phenomenon was something you could hide this technology behind. If you mixed up a little bit of truth with a whole range of disinformation you could get some of that stuff to stick. It was a very useful curtain behind which you could hide real secrets or real technology. So, yeah, you have to be aware of all of this stuff.

I think that consciousness, being a somewhat highly malleable thing, is prone to—when you feed all of this disinformation into this interface that I've been trying to describe here with you and in my BICS essay—that interface becoming in a sense bent out of shape by a range of different inputs, such as the human input, which is characterized, in this case, by misinformation and disinformation from intelligence communities.

Mishlove: Nick, where do you think things are going from here? Do you have any sense of the future of this investigation?

Cook: In my own field, coming out of that aerospace and defense background, I recognize that a huge breakthrough has been made with this 2021 UAP study that was delivered to Congress by the Office of the Defense and Intelligence Community. People are going to sit up and take notice. Sadly, in the defense and intelligence realm, this is now going to be a thing. I regret to say that I think there will probably be some form of race to uncover some of the darker aspects of this among the great rival bloc powers. China, Russia, the United States, my own country, the UK, and I think others will be racing to try to understand what all of this means. Sadly, again, I think they will look through a prism or lens and see this in terms of weapons technology and advances in the field of intelligence gathering and what have you.

We've seen this in the past with remote viewing, which came out of the Cold War race between the Soviet Union and the United States to gain a psychic upper hand between themselves. I'm a little fearful that that race now triggered by this UAP study might be a race to acquire technology that would replicate UFO-UAP type platforms; that's the vernacular in the defense world.

That is why it's going to be incredibly important for all of science to get engaged in this, not just defense science. This is a phenomenon that deserves to be understood and to be made as transparent as possible. The last thing that any of us wants is to see an esoteric arms race in this area. That is not what it is about. I think based on my own explorations of this subject, and perhaps, dare I say it, your own too, Jeff, it's a subject that is not to be suborned by any particular interest group. Consciousness is something that we need to explore for the greater good of humanity. That is really only going to come through transparency and the whole of science engaging in this because it is so elusive that only by the whole of science approaching it, are we going to make any progress in chipping away at it.

Mishlove: I have a hypothesis I'd like to share with you. I think the universe itself is conscious.

Cook: Of course, me too.

Mishlove: When you, for example, put out the intention that you wanted to meet with the world leaders of consciousness research, and then out of the blue you got a two-year grant to do exactly that, I think it was the universe responding to your intention.

Cook: Thank you, and that is the way, funnily enough, I see it as well. I read and hugely enjoyed your own BICS essay section about metaphysical realism—the idea that the universe itself is conscious, responsive, and alive. I have prodded it enough, I hope in a nice way, to know that that is true. You put the intention out there, and if the intention aligns with, for simplicity sake, let's call it a greater good, the universe will respond—in that sense, consciousness will respond. Of course, that is unexplained.

That is so mysterious that it can do that, but there are enough instances of it in your case, as in my case. We all know people who have done that, and the universe has in some way responded. Let's test that in a more widespread way and look at what will happen if whole communities can put out that positive intention. We are at a perilous point in humanity's evolution. We are faced with existential threats like climate change. We seem to have regressed, unfortunately, in a national security setting to something that equates to a Cold War mentality. The more that this intention can be put out there to explore consciousness in a positive way, hopefully, the more the universe will respond in a positive way back. That's my hope and dream for the future.

Mishlove: Nick Cook, this has been a delightful conversation. It's very exciting for me to have it with someone with your background in the aerospace and defense industries and technology. It adds a whole new layer for me and the *New Thinking Allowed* audience. Thank you so much for being with me.

Cook: Thank you for having me on as a guest.

3

Alien Encounters
with
Ralph Blumenthal

⌣

Jeffrey Mishlove: Today we'll be exploring alien contacts and abductions with my guest Ralph Blumenthal, a long time reporter for the *New York Times*. He is also author of *The Believer: Alien Encounters, Hard Science and the Passion of John Mack*. Welcome Ralph, it's a pleasure to be with you once again.

Ralph Blumenthal: Thank you, Jeff. A pleasure to be with you.

Mishlove: We're going to be focusing today on alien abductions and contacts, the very thing that captivated the interest of John Mack, whom you wrote about in your book, *The Believer*. I think a good place to start would be with the famous Betty and Barney Hill case.

Blumenthal: This was the mother lode of abductions. Interestingly enough, it happened in 1961 but it didn't come out until about five years later because Betty and Barney Hill kept it secret. Betty and Barney Hill were an interracial, New Hampshire couple; interesting for that time in the 1960s. Betty was white; Barney was black. He was a postal worker who had been a World War II combat soldier and Betty was a social worker. They were a very good couple, very close, and they were involved in civil rights work in New Hampshire which made them nervous about telling their story.

In 1961 they took off on a belated honeymoon to Niagara Falls, Canada but a storm came in and so they cut short the honeymoon. On the way back they noticed this craft, or something that looked like a plane at first, following them. It was late at night, and the roads were deserted. They got increasingly nervous as they got a good glimpse of what looked like a huge craft with windows. They stopped their car in the middle of the road but then they blocked out a lot of the event, only recovering their memory of it later. They remembered some parts consciously, which is typical for these abduction scenarios, but other details only came out later in hypnotic regressions. They had a very good psychiatrist, Benjamin Simon, who had done remarkable work in World War II with traumatized veterans, so he knew what he was doing when he came across traumatized people.

A book was written about it called *The Interrupted Journey* and there was a movie. What they captured during these hypnotic regressions was that they were experimented upon by alien beings aboard a ship. Betty's dress was torn as they tried to get it off. The dress was later found torn. Barney's shoes were scraped as he remembered being pulled across the ground into the ship. That was basically it. They told their story to what they thought was a church audience, a very limited group, but there was a reporter in the room. He tried to get them to tell their story. They declined but he wrote the story anyway in the *Boston Herald Traveler*, and it was a sensation.

It really is the first big abduction case. There were earlier cases—one in Brazil—and a lot of other strange stories over the years, but this was the first one that came up in the mass media era. John Mack became aware of it much later because he didn't get into the subject until about 1990.

Mishlove: I actually met Betty Hill.

Blumenthal: Oh wow.

Mishlove: It was very interesting. I don't think I've shared this with you before, Ralph, but while I was a graduate student at Berkeley, one of my professors in my interdisciplinary PhD program in parapsychology was James Harder [1926-2006], who was the research director for the Aerial Phenomena Research Organization. He had hypnotized the victims from these early abduction cases.

Blumenthal: "Victims" is a good word because many of them did feel deeply traumatized. Although John Mack found a positive element to these experiences. The abductees—or the experiencers as he preferred to call them—emerged with a greater appreciation for the fate of the earth, working against pollution, and for the love that they felt permeates the universe. They felt really attracted to these beings as god figures. Betty went on to live quite a few years without Barney who died some years after the experiences. She claimed, near the end of her life, that she was able to call these UFOs; she could initiate contact, which is quite controversial to say. It was viewed as fringy, but the whole story is crazy to begin with, so who can say what part is crazier than another part?

John Mack realized that these stories held up under repeated interviews. There was no physical proof—proof was always lacking—but the mindset of the people telling the stories and the witness statements corroborating the accounts were very convincing to him. Betty was quite a personality in her own right for many years after the event.

Mishlove: I met her at James Harder's home one day, back when I was a graduate student. He invited me over and there she was.

Blumenthal: Did she talk about the experience?

Mishlove: It was really a brief encounter, but yes.

Blumenthal: Wow. She donated all the artifacts of that day to the University of New Hampshire at Durham for people to study. It includes her torn dress, Barney's shoes; all the videotapes and audiotapes of their hypnotic regressions. The skeptics debunk these stories out of reflex by saying, "Well, it's impossible because …" Of course it's impossible. No one doubts that it's impossible, yet these people say it happened and there's some credibility to their stories.

Let the skeptics go through the archive, listen to the tapes. I've listened to a lot of experiencer tapes myself, but not from that case particularly. Like John Mack, I have to conclude that there is no better explanation than what the people themselves say happened, which may not be very good but it's the only thing there is.

Mishlove: The Betty and Barney Hill experience seem to be the first milestone, as it were, of what became a social movement. By the time John Mack got involved there were already organizations for the abductees.

Blumenthal: Right, they had come together. As I say in the book, Budd Hopkins had started researching this some years before John Mack ever got into it. He was really the first big researcher along with David Jacobs. Budd Hopkins was an artist on Cape Cod who had witnessed a UFO on the way to a party and got interested in the subject. He found, not only were the UFOs interesting, but also the people who said they were taken by beings from the UFOs. Budd Hopkins thought that people wouldn't care what an artist thinks; he didn't have a career to risk. Then he got David Jacobs involved, who did have a career to risk. He was a professor at Temple University who had written a groundbreaking book on the history of UFOs. Together they performed hypnosis on, and interviewed, their own experiencers. By the time John Mack got into it, the phenomenon was well underway.

Mishlove: There's also James Harder. He didn't write any books, so he didn't achieve that kind of a profile, and worked rather quietly. He was a hydraulic engineering professor at Berkeley and a practicing hypnotist who was usually on the scene right away. He hypnotized, if I recall correctly, Travis Walton and the victims of the Pascagoula case. He was very quietly establishing for himself, and for the organization that he was part of—called the Aerial Phenomena Research Organization— an understanding of what was going on. I think he wanted to avoid publicity in order not to taint the data if there were future abductees.

Blumenthal: Right, unlike John Mack who welcomed and relished the publicity. Mack was a very charismatic guy who was ready for the fight when it came from Harvard and from others. He was not intimidated. On the contrary, he was energized. There were a lot of other researchers who have not gotten the same amount of publicity, perhaps because they weren't psychiatrists at Harvard, which was a big factor in his fame or infamy. He wasn't just a UFO researcher but an eminent leader in the field of mental health.

There were many others doing the research, you're absolutely right, and they were coming up with different things. In the book I talk about a big conference at MIT that John Mack went to in 1992 where people from different disciplines compared notes. There were psychiatrists like him, atomic physicists and theologians, and all of them were coming up with something slightly different, like the proverbial blind men and the elephant. It's a very strange phenomenon that has a basic symmetry to it, which attracted John Mack. He saw that all the stories were consistent, or they rhymed maybe. The details were wildly different in many cases so different researchers were getting different information. The researcher you mentioned possibly had a different take than John Mack.

Mishlove: As I recall from the work I did with Harder, he felt that he had a real understanding of the alien population. He explained to me, for example, that they had 20,000 members in their species and that they had life spans of roughly 20,000 years. He seemed to feel that by quietly interviewing people he was learning a good deal about who these visitors were.

Blumenthal: That is a really interesting point. I don't really get into that in my book because it was hard enough focusing on John Mack and the stories he was getting. Since then more information has come out; different experiencers have been emboldened, probably through John Mack's notoriety and his courage to come forward. I just got an email from someone who wrote a book about what happened to her. People are talking about the different races not just the so-called Grays—the short little figures with the mushroom colored skin, big eyes, and rubbery kind of physique. Those are the common alien types that you see depicted in movies, books, and illustrations, but there are many others like doctor types and taller more humanoid figures. They may come from different corners of the cosmos or at different stages of development. The whole thing is so crazy—even to talk about it is mind-boggling. You have to have a certain amount of courage just to wade into this field and listen to what these people are saying.

Mishlove: One of the points that you made is that Betty Hill claimed after her abduction that she was able to invoke, somehow, the presence of UFOs. There's a group of people or a cult of people, who also believe they can invoke these phenomena.

Blumenthal: One of the major mysteries in the whole field is why some people are taken and other people are not. John Mack looked at the population of people who spoke to him, some of whom were very reluctant, and he found there was absolutely nothing to distinguish them. They were not mentally ill; they were not delusionary; they were ordinary people from all different walks of life. They were not rape victims looking to transfer their rape experience to aliens. Nothing like that. If they were all basically "normal" people, why were they picked and other people were not? That's something I focus on in my book.

It may have to do with some structure in the brain, or some physical abnormality that has yet to be detected, that enables some people to connect with this other dimension. There may be some ability they have, a psychic ability, or some chemical interaction that enables them to connect and others unable to. Then it would follow that some could bring on these contacts, as many of them say they're able to do. I spoke to an experiencer who said he feels some ability to connect, or at least he knows when *they* are coming. He feels a certain energy in the room and a hum and all these signals. Betty may have been on to something. She was widely ridiculed for saying she could call in UFOs but everything else she said was wild, too.

Mishlove: Back in 1976 I did a study with a UFO contactee who claimed he had been abducted, and that aliens had operated on his brain, giving him strange powers. He said he could produce UFOs on demand and he did. He predicted that there would be a UFO, it would be seen by hundreds of people, photographed, and that the photograph would be published in the front page of one of the local newspapers in the San Francisco Bay Area. That actually happened within days.

Blumenthal: That's another example of the information that these entities are able to convey. They tell you when the UFOs are coming in and to look for them and sure enough they'll be there. This ability to know the future is one of the hallmarks of these experiences.

Mishlove: One of the individuals who has been prominent in the UFO scene is Dr. Steven Greer, who has launched a movement for people to invoke lights in the sky or UFOs, as did Ted Owens, the man I studied for so many years. I wonder, did Dr. Mack have any interactions with Greer?

Blumenthal: I don't believe so. I think Greer came along later. I'm trying to think back to whether Mack talked about people who had the ability to call the UFOs. I don't think so, although it came up in some of the stories. I know that Steven Greer has organized these camping expeditions where they see these lights materialize. It does seem to happen to people who are open to it more than other people for some reason. Also, it seems to run in families. John Mack found that if you've had an abduction experience it's likely that your parents and your grandparents did, and likely your children will. This was a point of terror to some people knowing that the encounters they had would be inflicted on their children as well. They were powerless to protect their children.

Why would aliens focus on families? Is it a matter of studying a family line? Also, the phenomenon seemed to focus on people in their reproductive years. If you haven't been abducted by menopause, chances are you won't be. It does seem to be related to reproduction, although children as young as two years old relate these experiences of flying up in the sky. They were too young to have read books about it or to see movies, so where these stories came from is anybody's guess. Mack concluded that these children were abducted because there was no other way for these kids to know about it. They weren't making it up because the stories were so consistent. I'm not surprised to hear that Steven Greer and others have been interested in the ability to make contact at will.

Mishlove: Another aspect of the whole scene around UFOs is the cattle mutilations. It's been researched extensively by Linda Moulton Howe. I wonder if Dr. Mack looked into that at all?

Blumenthal: Somebody asked him that at a conference and he said he had his hands full with the abductions. At that point he was not about to go into these other anomalous events, of which there were many. Later on in his career he did explore many other examples of anomalous events including crop circles and survival of consciousness, if you want to call it that. But, at the time, he stayed away from cattle mutilations because he had enough trouble with Harvard over alien contacts.

There's the whole story about Skinwalker Ranch which Robert Bigelow, the billionaire Las Vegas space entrepreneur and hotel mogul, bought. This is a ranch in Utah that had so scared the owners, a very well-grounded couple who witnessed all these strange things happen, that they finally fled. Bigelow's organization conducted a bunch of experiments there and they set up all kinds of cameras. Among the many spooky, unexplained events that take place at this ranch were these cattle mutilations. Calves and cows would be found, in the morning, cut as if with a knife and their insides neatly removed. There were theories that there were vampire bats,animals, or coyotes, but none of that seems a satisfactory explanation for the precision of these cuts. It's completely eerie.

Linda Moulton Howe and others have really made a specialty of investigating these mutilations. Law enforcement has been notified because it's affected ranchers' livelihoods. They would understand if the cattle were killed by bears or wolves, but killed in this completely bizarre way is another aspect of this unfolding mystery.

Mishlove: As I recall, in some instances the cattle were killed in the winter when there was snow on the ground and there were no tracks to be found leading up to the cattle, that an animal or a human would have necessarily had to have made in the snow.

Blumenthal: "Skinwalker" is a Navajo term for shape-shifting entities that the Navajo believe are part of the spiritual dimension that are invisible but that intrude on our reality. There were stories of the original owners of the ranch who encountered gigantic wolves. When they shot them the wolves wouldn't die; they would walk away. The farmer sent his son back to get a more powerful rifle and he shot the wolf again and again but it walked away. One theory was that the wolf was a spiritual being that couldn't be killed because it wasn't alive. That's only one of the extremely spooky things that happened at the Skinwalker Ranch and cattle mutilation was definitely part of it.

Mishlove: So the implication both with the UFO abductions and with the cattle mutilations seems to be that there are entities, who live in another dimension of space and they're able to enter into our dimension and then leave without going through the normal procedures that any three-dimensional creature would have to go through.

Blumenthal: This is what Mack had to contend with. Where did these things come from? They materialize in the room, often at night, sometimes in broad daylight and when people are driving cars. In one case, a woman was on her snowmobile and blacked out, later finding her clothes neatly folded next to her. She recalled an abduction experience during a regression. John Mack frequently said that this phenomenon has a way of penetrating our reality.

Hopkins and Jacobs took a somewhat different view saying it *was* happening in our reality and these were real experiences—as real as anything else people encounter—and the abductions were for purposes of producing a hybrid race. John Mack drifted away from that later because it's not that clear that it's happening in everyday reality because if it was we'd see it. It's got to be happening in some other dimensional reality which we don't understand. That doesn't mean it's not happening and it's not real to these people.

Every time Mack turned up at a conference, or later at Harvard when he was under investigation, there were people who said, "Oh, I can explain this. This is sleep paralysis. This is a mental illness." He effectively demolished that kind of debunking because they hadn't studied the material as he had. He kept saying, "If someone has a good explanation I'd like to hear it. I'm not wedded to my explanation, flawed as it is. But I haven't heard anything better." That's what we're left with, even after all these years.

Mishlove: As I recall, early on in the abduction scene there were women in particular who felt that they had been impregnated and that they had lost the child or the child had been removed from them; it was being raised by alien entities in another location or another dimension; they would be brought to visit the child from time to time. I'm under the impression that, at least initially, Mack was willing to accept these stories at face value.

Blumenthal: He was very taken with these stories. He played an audio tape at Harvard of a woman, during a hypnosis session, recalling the removal of her fetus. She was weeping, cursing and shaking with fright as she recalled this years and years later. It made a very powerful impression on him but I don't know whether he took it at face value. As far as I'm aware, nobody has been able to produce gynecological evidence from a doctor, that this woman was indisputably pregnant and then suddenly, without a miscarriage or a birth, the fetus disappeared. There are many stories of women recounting this but no evidence to back it up, because that's everyone's first reaction. Didn't she have a doctor's examination? What did the doctor say? Did the doctor find her pregnant and then the next day find her not pregnant? That missing evidence is among the most dramatic that you would expect to find if this was happening in reality.

But what makes the story more powerful is that these women, some of whom told Mack that they never had had sex, and yet, they felt that they were pregnant, that they were abducted, the fetus was removed, that they had to accept that fact willingly. In other words, it was not a forced procedure where they were compelled to submit to the removal of the fetus, but it was something that they had to agree to do willingly for the future of the race or something like that. Then, on a subsequent abduction, they were shown their hybrid offspring. The book Budd Hopkins wrote had many other accounts of women, and men, who were shocked later to see and to be told of their hybrid child. Some children were not doing well; they were sickly because of the mixture of species.

There were many accounts of this nature confronting John Mack. Where are all these hybrids if they exist? Are they walking around as David Jacobs suggested in a book he wrote, *Walking Among Us*? Wouldn't tests show that they differ from ordinary human beings? I spoke to somebody who said he believed he was a hybrid and yet tests showed him as no different from anybody else; his DNA and blood tests were normal. Are the aliens that clever enough that they can make hybrid beings look like everybody else? Where does this take us?

Mishlove: I find it interesting that these stories seem to have many common elements. I imagine Mack looked into whether the myth is pretty common in the culture or whether the people who repeat these stories are actually quite independent of it.

Blumenthal: Mack realized pretty quickly that the stories had a basic similarity, a consistency. People would be doing whatever they do normally, whether it's going to sleep or driving a car or walking in the fields and then they would become aware of a UFO. They would see it land and then their memories would become hazy. They might consciously remember some parts like seeing beings emerge but often that memory was suppressed and they would recall it only later. Then we can talk about hypnosis as a controversial factor in whether these ideas can be implanted.

The symmetry of these stories made him believe that these people were saying something that people were familiar with. On the other hand, the details were so different. I spoke to an experiencer who told me about encounters with grasshopper-type beings or mantis-type beings that he had met many times in his life. His memories were clear enough to recall them very well. The insectoid beings don't come up very often. Other people have seen reptilian beings. This may go back to what you said before about different alien races that people say they have encountered. It's not just the small, so-called Grays, which may be robotic according to some descriptions. They may not even be living creatures at all because they seem to serve other tall and more commanding figures.

Mishlove: We were talking about the commonality of the reports. Another area that seems very intriguing is a question of implants. I know a medical doctor, Roger Leir, who has written a book, was removing these implants. So there's quite a large lore around the implants. Whitley Strieber maintains that he had an implant put in that has provided him with certain telepathic abilities.

Blumenthal: That's another problematic area. I am not aware of any object being removed from an experiencer that tested credibly as an alien structure, implement or device. I tell in my book the story of somebody who remembered being implanted with a device. It had protruded from his body and he took it out and sent it for testing. An atomic physicist at MIT named Dave Prichard, who was very involved in this research, tested it using all kinds of sophisticated chronograph tests. He concluded that it was a biological object that grew in the body. Are the aliens so smart that they are able to construct an implant that passes as a human piece of tissue? Just the way UFOs appear and disappear at will, or seem to at some times, the phenomena also seem to appear and disappear. People have very vivid memories of being implanted with a small BB-sized device, or women have things put inside their bodies and they remember the instruments with great detail. Yet, when scientists later search for these objects it's not clear that they find them or that they pass muster as alien technology.

Again it's part of the mystery. There's a trickster element here. These things appear and then they disappear. John Mack said he had a wand that an experiencer gave him from one of these beings. Mack never produced it. If we could have an ashtray from a UFO then we'll know they're real. That's the problem. These things exist in some kind of a parallel universe or some subtle realm where they evade proof again and again. People set up cameras at night to try to catch them, but they don't come out.

There was one experiment at Skinwalker Ranch that I found very haunting. They had two cameras set up to capture pictures of these strange things, strange beings and all kinds of really spooky phenomena that were showing up at night. The cameras were positioned so that one would be visible to the other. In the morning, they went to check the cameras and one camera was completely destroyed with all the insides ripped out of it. The other camera, which was focused on it, showed nothing happening to that camera at all. Even when you go through these really rigorous scientific procedures to try to capture this phenomenon you're left holding the bag, and it's the same way with the implants. I'm not aware of any implant that resolves the issue. If there were, I probably would know about it.

Mishlove: Ralph, you're one of the people, along with your partner Leslie Kean, who broke the story in the *New York Times* about UFO sightings captured on radar and video by the US Navy. These are pretty hardcore physical sightings. Do you think that what you reported on is related in any way to the abduction phenomenon? Or could these be completely separate?

Blumenthal: That's an interesting question. You could say it's a step in the direction of understanding anomalous phenomena. The article we wrote for the *New York Times* was only about UFOs, or UAPs as the military prefers to call them, Unidentified Aerial Phenomena. We didn't write about aliens at all or alien abduction because the science is only up to confirming the presence of unidentified objects that have a physicality. Now we know they do, for the first time. They were written about for many years as possible spiritual things or people's imagination or that seemed to float in and out of existence. They were captured on radar, they've been eyeballed by jet pilots, they're captured on thermal imaging devices, so they are, as far as we can say with some certainty now, physical. Where do they come from? Are they intelligent? Who's piloting them? Are they from outer space? They've been seen going into and emerging from the ocean. They have an inter-media aspect where they can also function underwater, which seems even more amazing than that they're up in the skies. You can imagine things flying around in the skies—it's hard to imagine things operating equally well underwater.

We can say that there's a physicality to these things: they exist; we don't know more than that. That's a far cry from aliens and intelligent beings. There is not the same level of physical confirmation as we have for UFOs.

Mishlove: Many of the alien abduction reports do include marks on the ground where landings supposedly took place.

Blumenthal: You're right about that. There are a number of physical confirmations that Mack was very attracted to. There have been marks on the ground where people have seen UFOs land on the ground (*sic*) there sometimes seems to have strange conditions. The snow melts there first; the grass doesn't grow there the way it grows on other parts of the field. So, yes, that's another physical confirmation. People have also remembered being abducted and then coming back with so-called scoop marks or scars where supposed experiments were conducted on them. I just became aware of a whole different phenomenon which may or may not be related called the "red grid" marks phenomenon. People have pinpoints in the shape of a square on any part of the skin. It doesn't seem to be related necessarily to abduction because people have red grid marks that don't remember being abducted. Where these marks come from is another mystery.

There's a group of people who exhibit this phenomenon who are trying to figure out the commonalities. What distinguishes them from other people? As I said, some have mentioned abduction experiences; many others have not. In one case John Mack had a quadriplegic who had marks on his body that he could not have inflicted upon himself. Many seem to be the so-called scoop marks, as if a little bit of skin was lifted out for testing. Whitley Strieber has very eloquently described these experiences.

Another aspect of physical confirmation attracted John Mack. He said in some cases there were witnesses. I spoke to an experiencer who said his partner saw some of his experience. She witnessed an energy in the room, a hum, and something strange going on. Look at Betty and Barney Hill—did both people have mutual delusions? This is what troubled the psychiatrist who investigated the case, Ben Simon. How did two people come up with the same story? This mystery is really intractable and it's not easily debunked, despite what the so-called skeptics say.

Mishlove: Ralph Blumenthal, this has been once again a fascinating probe into, as you say, an unsolved mystery. It may be related to many other unsolved mysteries. I think if we were to look at the whole range of what some people call Forteana, or phenomena that defy conventional explanation, there would be many dozens if not hundreds of other examples. It's very important that we pay attention to these anomalies. I want to thank you once again very much for sharing your knowledge.

Blumenthal: It's a real pleasure Jeff, love to do it. Thank you for inviting me.

4

Human Encounters with Aliens: Part 1: Abductions and the Western Paradigm with John Mack

Mishlove: Today we will be exploring human encounters with aliens. This is Part one of a two-part series with Dr. John Mack, a professor of psychiatry at Harvard University's Cambridge Hospital. Dr. Mack is a Pulitzer Prize-winning author of a book titled *A Prince of Our Disorder*, which is a biography of T.E. Lawrence, Lawrence of Arabia. He is also the author of *Abduction: Human Encounters with Aliens*. Welcome, John.

Mack: It's good to be here, Jeff.

Mishlove: It's a pleasure to be with you. Traditionally in psychiatry, if a patient were to come to you and report that they'd had contact with alien creatures, it would be almost automatically assumed, I think, that this person is likely to be psychotic.

Mack: That was my initial reaction when I first heard about this type of case. A colleague of mine, a woman psychologist, asked me if I would like to meet with Budd Hopkins. This was the fall of 1989, and I said, "Who's he?" which showed how little I knew about this subject at that time. She said, "He's an artist in New York who works with people who report being taken by alien beings into spacecraft." I said, "Oh, he must be mad if he takes that seriously. This must be some new form of mental illness." She said, "No, no, it's very serious. Do you want to meet him?"

Rather reluctantly, I agreed to meet with him one day in New York—January 10, 1990, a day that changed my life in certain ways. What struck me about what Budd Hopkins had to say, aside from the fact that he was not mad at all, but a very intelligent, thoughtful, discriminating, and caring person, were the accounts of, at that point, close to two hundred people that had had very similar experiences. These people were, as far as I could tell, of sound mind. They described, in great detail, that they had been taken, on beams of light generally, by alien beings out of their homes, cars, in the case of one woman from a snowmobile, and children from schoolyards. They were three-and-a-half to four-foot alien beings—that was the most commonly described variety—into spacecraft, and subjected to invasive procedures.

These people did not know each other and they reported their experiences very reluctantly. He had written an article about an abduction case that drew them to him. They didn't want to believe it themselves. As far as I could tell—and this has become clearly established, having now worked with ninety such people—there was no apparent psychiatric illness that could account for this. In spite of what people say, "Well, there was a lot about this in the media, and they may have picked it up," these are not people that had been particularly exposed to media accounts. In any case, they were reporting many, many details that were not in the media but were consistent among the people that I've worked with.

Mishlove: What you've just said obviously raises many, many questions, and I'm bubbling with questions to ask you, but the first one that I want to come back to: you use the word "spacecraft." How would they or you know that what they saw was actually a spacecraft?

Mack: Sometimes the person has not seen the spacecraft, but often they have. In a number of these cases, they're floated through the wall of their home, through the window, or through the door. Again, so many of the details of these experiences make no sense in our Newtonian, Cartesian, Western—whatever you want to call it—notions of reality. Yet, the stories are consistently described with, again, the self-critical attitude that the people have. They may see a typical unidentified flying object, a saucer-shaped or cigar-shaped vehicle on the ground near their home, emanating bright lights, or they may be taken by a small craft up into the sky to a kind of mother ship, which they see very clearly. Many of them actually see the UFOs, and the insides are so uniformly described as rounded, curved walls, with complicated instrument panels, that it's become clear that this is some kind of craft in the sky, which they would naturally call a spacecraft.

Mishlove: I think people would naturally draw that inference, but to me it's still an inference. I think you might agree, we don't really know exactly what these things are.

Mack: Fair enough. This gets into the way of how we know anything, or our use of language, but we call something which is seen in the sky and which seems to be moving from one place to another, a spacecraft. This has to do with where our own technology has come to. It could be virtual reality that appears similar to what we already know as an airplane or a certain type of aerospace vehicle, so we call it a spacecraft. But if you want to get down to the very core of the way language structures reality for us, you could even question whether they're spacecraft.

Mishlove: You've described, in your book, cases that were reported back in the 19th century of people who talked about airships.

Mack: The article is by Jerome Clark, who's been a student of the UFO phenomenon for many years. He looked back at the newspaper accounts during the airship craze of the last decade of the nineteenth century. Many of those illustrations looked like balloons, or the technology of the time. But he went further than that. He did an exhaustive search of all of the photographs and the descriptions he could find, and, lo and behold, many of them did appear very much like the current, modern-day UFO. The people of the time did not have the technological knowledge to describe them as what they were. So he concluded that these were probably UFOs not so different from what we're seeing now. The nineteenth century perceptual development hadn't reached the point where they could be perceived the way we now think they are. Again, you're raising the question whether even that is actual or constructed reality.

Mishlove: We could take this in so many different directions, but let's go back further into the past, because the accounts don't just begin even in the 19th century, do they?

Mack: If you go back into the early times there is Ezekiel's wheel from the bible—which now many ufologists think was a UFO—or chariots seen in the sky. Go back to the fairies that kidnapped people in Ireland and other countries. There are some similarities, but you're dealing with oral traditions, and it's an easy leap of mind to say, "Well, we've had this going on all through the centuries and through the millennia even." The problem is the methods of knowing then are so different from current knowledge. To compare a phenomenon you have to use more or less the same investigative method, and our methods and perceptual capabilities now are so different.

The people that were reporting those experiences weren't being studied clinically. When somebody's had an unusual experience, or something that doesn't fit, or you want to investigate, you talk to that person in great detail, or you speak to other witnesses to find out what they've seen. We now have a body of investigative tradition that can document what's going on. From that point of view this appears to have some distinct features. It also appears—now I'm getting more into my own kind of sense of this—that this thing is entering into our reality in a more hard-edged way.

The first case that we have is that of Betty and Barney Hill, the interracial couple that was coming back from their vacation in Montreal, and who saw a craft that emanated this bright light. They actually saw and were confronted by these creatures. They were terrified. They were taken in and each reports various experiments that were done on their bodies—skin scrapings, probings—and the accounts compare. Since that time more and more cases are being reported, and it appears that the phenomenon is occurring with greater frequency now than in the past, but, again, we don't know that. There may be reasons for the increased frequency; if that's so, then why? We're still trying to establish how distinct is this from earlier reports.

Mishlove: The Betty and Barney Hill case was made into a motion picture and a very popular book back in the 1960s.

Mack: That's right, the movie came out in the mid-1970s, with James Earl Jones playing Barney Hill.

Mishlove: You're a professor of psychiatry at Harvard. You mention that when you first heard about Budd Hopkins, who was an amateur researcher into that phenomenon, you wondered whether *he* was crazy. Now you're doing clinical work yourself. How do your colleagues accept this?

Mack: The range is extraordinary, as I have, on the one hand, a very prominent astrophysicist colleague at Harvard who has become a kind of comrade-in-arms. He's gone on record saying that he believes that the work of people like Ken Ring, who works with near-death experiencers, and myself in this area, will teach us more about the nature of the cosmos than anything scientists will discover using telescopes to explore the heavens. It goes from that end to the acting chair of my department saying, "I wish John weren't doing this." In between are all kinds of people who array themselves. I have received letters of support from psychiatrists who have seen similar cases or say, "Continue it. This is good work," to people that think I've gone off some kind of deep end.

Mishlove: The obvious counter-hypothesis may be a sociological one, that this is a myth in the making, that there's a belief system that is somehow being engendered in the subconscious mind within the culture itself, perhaps like a new religion, or some other sort of social movement.

Mack: That's quite consistent with what I'm finding, because increasingly folklorists like Peter Rojcewicz and Thomas Eddie Bullard, are looking back into myth-making, and seeing, what was the experiential reality or the kernel of truth in the physical world. That is, what did people actually see and experience from which myths came? We have this notion in the West that a myth is an invented imagining which comes out of the psyche in some way. This is a very culture-centered notion of myth; culture-centered in terms of what our culture would tend to see. What they're finding is that there may have been visitations, or that there are actual physical bases for the myth. In that sense, a myth or a religion could evolve from this, but that doesn't go against the idea that something physical, something actual, is occurring in our material universe.

Mishlove: So what you're saying is, if we're going to look at this we have to be willing to approach it with a certain subtlety of mind, not to jump to conclusions one way or the other, but to be able to entertain simultaneously perhaps several hypotheses. Maybe many different levels of phenomena are interacting with each other at once, so there isn't going to be any kind of clear-cut way of looking at it.

Mack: Exactly. I often get asked questions like, "Well, is this real? Is it not real?" or "Is this really going on?" or "Do you believe these people, or don't you? Are they telling the truth, or are they not?" All that kind of binary, linear thinking. The subtlety you're talking about is very to the point. In other words, we're not great on ambiguity, paradox, subtlety, and embracing the mystery and learning from it. I think this is an authentic mystery, and I think we learn from saying, "I don't know," and having what the Buddhists call the cleared zero mind before looking at it.

I agree with you. I think it is subtle. It may be that, for example, this may originate in some other dimension— the etheric world, or whatever you want to call that other dimension—and then they cross over and manifest in the physical world. We're not used to thinking that way. I think one of the purposes of the book, in a sense, is to open us to those widening notions of consciousness and reality.

Mishlove: You wrote a very eloquent passage about your communications over much of your life with Thomas Kuhn, the great historian of science who wrote the book *The Structure of Scientific Revolutions*. Could you talk about your discussions with him?

Mack: I was lucky to have known Tom Kuhn since I was a child. His parents and mine were friends, and I used to spend time with him in New York at Christmas time, so it was a natural thing to look him up in Cambridge. He's been at MIT where we had some really interesting conversations. He's the person that originated this term *paradigm*, or *paradigm change*, which has become a cliche, but it's indispensable for looking at how ideas grow, develop, and shift. I said, "Tom, I think I've got one here." In other words, there's something I don't think I can understand within my framework of reality. I was raised in a very materialist household. Materialist not in the sense of property acquisition, but in the sense that all that's real is the physical world, and everything else belongs to the subjective or the spiritual, that are studied in anthropology, psychology, religion, or abnormal psychology. But here is something, which seems to cross over from the subjective world, and shows up in the objective world. I didn't know what to do with that. I told him about this, and he gave me two pieces of advice. He said, "Don't worry about science, because science has become a new religion in this culture, that restricts reality to that which can be measured and observed with the senses. If you're going to talk about knowing beyond that, you need to have an expanded way of knowing." The other was, "Watch out for language, because language will trap you in structures of reality, so look out for certain dualisms like exists/doesn't exist, real/unreal, inside/outside, happened/didn't happen, because they will immediately polarize the debate."

What he suggested was to collect raw information and put aside language categories as much as possible. We can't do that completely. We're all creatures of the culture in which we're raised, but I try as best I can to suspend all those categories and stay with the ambiguity, the paradox, the uncertainty. The book is filled with paradox, filled with uncertainty, filled with "on the one hand/on the other hand," but that isn't necessarily getting received that way.

I can't say this is in our reality, or it's in this other reality. I don't know where it is. Something powerful and extraordinary is happening to these people, and they are of sound mind, and they don't believe it. It shatters their notions of reality, and yet it is occurring to them in ways that I can't account for as a psychiatrist in any other way but that what they say is occurring.

With all the alternative hypotheses that have been thrown at me, usually by people who have never really sat down and worked with this population, neither I nor anyone in the field— and I always say this because I want to hear it, it still hasn't happened—not a single abduction case has revealed any other explanation. The people are examined, we try to break down their stories, cross-examine them, look for possible abuse or some kind of other trauma. Never has a case revealed anything other than what it is.

The reverse is true. Many people have come to therapists, including myself, with the idea that there was incest and abuse because there is a strong reproductive, sexual, and traumatic element in their stories. When we look into that, nothing happens. I mean, it doesn't work. Some therapists will bring in their families to cross-examine them and then cause terrible trouble for them by exploring potential abuse, but nothing has ever panned out. In several cases, at some point, the person remembered with or without a relaxation or hypnosis approach, a memory of a UFO, or the little beings coming out of the UFO. I'm thinking of one particular case where they became deeply affected, and the emotions returned. There are those kinds of cases where something that is first explored as something familiar, such as sexual abuse or rape, reveals the abduction story behind it, but not the other way around.

Mishlove: The issue of memory itself has become increasingly controversial. When these people are reporting their memories to you, what tools do you have [in order] to know how much weight you can give to a memory being an actual memory, as opposed to being some sort of a fantasy?

Mack: The so-called false memory, or doubting memories, is applied to situations, which are not of core significance to the individual. There's a study at Harvard where people who have been deeply traumatized—as the abductees have, in many cases—do have memory distortions, but not for the traumatic events. The memory around the traumatic events is highly accurate and reliable. The rest of their memories haven't become distorted and confused. There is no evidence for a false memory when relating very powerful traumatic events that are described with great conviction and great detail by people who are of otherwise sound mind and are reliable observers. That doesn't mean I know what the memory was, but it's not a false memory. It's not something concocted.

Mishlove: It sounds as if what you're saying is you're inclined to take these reports at face value.

Mack: I take them seriously but I don't have a way to account for them. I hear the people. They describe experiences in great detail that are so similar, one to another, and the only thing I know that acts like that is real experience. Face value is another matter, because you're saying that it implies that this is occurring literally in this physical world. That would have no place for something which came from some other realm, crossed over into our reality, and entered our reality in this complex way. It's powerfully real for these people. It affects them like any other trauma might, but there are many elements that are not simply traumatic, that can create really extraordinary human growth and transformational directions for these individuals.

Mishlove: In other words, in many cases the encounter with aliens seems to be a very beneficial one.

Mack: There are so many pitfalls and subtleties one has to look at. Beneficial implies that it's for us and it's good for us, or it's not good for us. I don't look at it in those terms. I think one has to step back and look at a larger framework.

Mishlove: I know in some of the cases you've reported, the patients regarded the aliens as mentors to them.

Mack: That can happen, but it may be that whatever the principle at work here is, it's not particularly interested in us. It may, for example—and this is consistent with a lot of the data—regard us as a cancer on the planet, a search-and-destroy species, which mows down with bulldozers everything it comes across, and tears the earth apart for resources and markets, and is a blight. It may be looking at us that way, and saying, "What are we going to do about this species?" It's not particularly good or bad for us; it may be trying to intervene in some way to arrest us. I'm not saying that's true, but there are ways you can look at it that have very little to do with us, but more to do with some larger principle because we're so out of harmony with our own world.

Mishlove: Obviously we're dealing with something of enormous complexity, and probably not just one phenomenon but several different phenomena that sometimes get lumped together. You seem to be saying that [in] a case in which a patient might seem to be having a beneficial experience, it might not be quite what it seems.

Mack: You have to distinguish what may be the individual's personal journey. First they acknowledge the trauma, then the experience, and then they grow experiencing a wider sense of identity and reality. They see that we're not alone, that there are other beings, other entities, intelligences that exist, that they have a relationship with, which may be a very profound, even spiritual connection. That may be their personal journey, but that may not be what this is about. We're not very good at having a cosmic perspective. We only know what the aliens may say to people, and how they grow, or are traumatized by the experience.

Mishlove: I know in the fiction of writers like Kurt Vonnegut there are some interesting cases where humans feel very touched by alien intervention. It seems very personal, and later on you learn in the story the object of the aliens was something totally removed from anything that was suspected by the humans.

Mack: It could be that "We don't mean to harm you, we're trying to help your planet survive, and we're connecting with you for a higher purpose," is a deception. I get suspicious of that interpretation because that's such an American way of thinking, "I'm not going to get conned by these guys." I almost trust the face value more than I trust an American interpretation of it. A face-value look at it would be that it is some kind of complex process of evolution of species and consciousness that is going on here whereas deception is more what we watch out for.

Mishlove: Dr. John Mack, we've raised more questions than we've been able to answer, but fortunately this is Part one of a two-part series. In the second part, we go into greater depth on some of the subtleties: dream experiences, potential past-life encounters with aliens, many of the other things that you've written about, including both the beneficial and the detrimental aspects of these contacts. Dr. Mack, thank you so much for being with me.

Mack: Thank you for having me, Jeff.

5

Human Encounters with Aliens: Part 2:
The Larger Context of Abductions
with
John Mack

Jeffrey Mishlove: This is Part two of a two-part series on "Human Encounters with Aliens." My guest, Dr. John Mack, is a professor of psychiatry at Harvard University's Cambridge Hospital. He is the author of *Abduction: Human Encounters with Aliens,* and he is also the author of a Pulitzer-Prize-winning book called *A Prince of Our Disorder,* which is a biography of T.E. Lawrence, Lawrence of Arabia. Welcome back again, John.

John Mack: Good to be back, Jeff.

Mishlove: We covered some of the phenomenology of your clinical work with people who reported various encounters, typically alien abductions, and we raised a number of questions as to what is the nature of reality itself. Were these dreams? Were these fantasies? Were these physical encounters? It seems as if they're occurring across quite a spectrum of experience.

I interviewed a physicist, Fred Alan Wolf, who is the author of a book called *The Dreaming Universe*, in which he looks at the Everett-Graham-Wheeler notion of the multiple-universe or multiple-reality interpretation of quantum physics. He suggests that according to this view, which is becoming a dominant interpretation of quantum physics, we might view dreams as being an actual physical space, and that the things that occur in dreams really, on some level, exist.

Mack: It may be that people, when they're dreaming, are tapping into some other reality that enters our world filled with meaning. The notion of multiple dimensions doesn't explain anything, but makes sense because this phenomenon cannot be explained from a purely four-dimensional, extraterrestrial universe. The argument that this isn't occurring because space vehicles would take too many years to get here from some other place is beside the point. If these beings have mastered technologies that are way beyond anything we now know, it's very possible that they can go through wormholes that collapse time, or that they can come from some other dimension and enter our universe by thought processes. There are all kinds of possibilities that scientists have conceived of, but which our technology hasn't even begun to approach. Rather than look upon this as extraterrestrial, I think it does make more sense to use Jacques Vallée's term, a 'multiverse', a universe of multiple dimensions from which these beings may come.

Mishlove: In other words, if the facts don't fit our current theories, it's not the facts that have to change, it's our theories.

Mack: What's happened to me so often as I've tried to speak about this phenomenon is that people try to force it into some sort of bed in which it will not fit and demand physical proof, rather than to expand their notions of reality. To take in something which, from the standpoint of our Western notions just can't exist, shatters our ideas of reality. But here is something that invites us to expand our ideas of what realities are possible.

Mishlove: I'd like to go over a few points that we covered in Part One. One of the questions that has come up is, when people in a clinical setting report to you their memories, how do you know that that memory is real as opposed to fantasy? You responded that there's good evidence to suggest that when people are reporting a trauma, that the trauma itself is real, even if other memories are not.

Mack: That's correct, but in this case there's also a whole other set of data which makes the idea of fantasy extraordinarily unlikely. These experiences are too similar, too consistent, too congruent among thousands, if not millions of people. According to some of the polls, people who have not been in touch with each other are reporting details that are not in the media. Fantasy isn't like that. Fantasy is highly individualized. People have complex narratives of being taken by alien beings with big black eyes—who were not known in the culture until recently—up through the air into spacecraft, and subjected to what seem like examinations. They report skin samples taken and reproductive procedures performed which involve taking sperm from men, eggs from women, reimplanting an altered egg, then pregnancies later. They've then been taken to see small hybrid beings on these ships. This is a whole elaborate narrative of experiences extraordinarily similar among thousands of people who have not been in touch with each other.

When people hear of others having this experience they are both shocked and relieved. They're shocked because they've considered it as a dream, as a fantasy, and then, when they realize other people have had the same experience, they know it's not their private fantasy. They're relieved because they know that somebody can listen to them and they're not crazy, although people sometimes would prefer to be crazy than to have this be real.

Mishlove: If I look at the literature of these things and talk to other therapists, I realize that there's a group of people who are dealing with alien abductions in a similar fashion to what you've described. There are groups of people dealing with Satanic ritual abuse, with past-life memories, with spirit possession, or with apparitions of the Virgin Mary, and they each have a certain coherence about them. Are we to take them all as equally credible?

Mack: I don't think we should accept anything as for sure and to be skeptical about everything. I'd like to define the word skeptical, because it's abused in this field. Skeptical means having an open mind, inquiring, looking into something, wondering, and not being sure. The way skeptical is used in this field means debunking, basically something doesn't fit our notions of reality, therefore it's not so. Skeptics are vigilantes of the Scientific, with a capital S, paradigm that we're in.

Mishlove: I couldn't agree with you more about the abuses that occur in the name of skepticism.

Mack: You mentioned a number of different areas of study, like Satanic abuse and we might include near-death experiences and past lives. There are many experiences that people are having which don't fit into our notions of reality. None of that is supposed to be true, or can't exist in our way of knowing, which is restricted by a certain methodology. You have to have proof and an observer, who's quite detached from the object of what he's studying using instruments or the senses. That's all that we can consider to be reality. Anything that comes from our whole psyche, or is investigated from the experiences of people, or the corroboration of experiences among different people, doesn't provide enough evidence in the scientific paradigm. There is physical corroboration for this phenomenon. It's not purely an experiential, psychological matter, but we have no place in our epistemology, for something like this.

I'll give you examples of the past life experience, because you mentioned that; and they're very illustrative. What often happens with the people that I work with is that when they relax during hypnosis they recall, say, an encounter with an alien being when they were a few days old. We're not supposed to be able to remember what happened when we were a few days old, because our notions of the brain don't allow that, but that doesn't prevent there being memories. The person will say, "Oh, I'm back here," meaning born into this culture, this physical world, again. At that point I have a choice. I can say, "Never mind you're back again. Tell me what happened when you were a baby, and then what did the aliens do, and what did your mother do?" Or I can pick up the word "back again," and say, "What do you mean, back again?"

I started to cue on those words and not ignore them. The person would say, "Well, I was here before."

"What do you mean, you were 'here before'?"

"I was a poet in England in the eighteenth century, and I ran afoul of the authorities." They would tell a very detailed story, which is told with just as much conviction as you and I would tell about our vacation or professional work event. The memories had extraordinary detail, and in a number of instances they were corroborated by other evidence. That isn't something I've been particularly out to prove.

Mishlove: Dr. Ian Stevenson of the University of Virginia.

Mack: He corroborated with actual occurrences, the stories of children who reported past lives, about events they could not know. One of the cases that is in the book, is about a young woman who knew almost nothing about ancient Egyptian culture and civilization who had an Egyptian past-life experience. She was a male court painter probably someplace between the Middle and the New Kingdom in Egypt. She knew how the paints were mixed, how they were made, and what the different dyes were like. That story came about because I picked up on the word "again," or "I'm back again." It really depends what we are able to learn, what we are capable of listening to and perceiving in our official reality. I don't use the word consensus anymore, because there is no consensus about what's reality.

Mishlove: Sure, if you talk to people in general, the consensus is very different from the "official" version.

Mack: I use the word official, but even that seems to be under some assault now. According to official reality, there are no past lives, there is no Satanic abuse, there are no near-death experiences. The last refuge of the Western scientific resistance is to call abductees liars. If you ever actually talked with them, you'd see that they're very sincere, straightforward, balanced, healthy people. I've had several of them tested psychologically. They're people of great integrity, and they didn't want to believe their experiences anymore—at first, at least—than anyone else would. They're very skeptical, in the sense we were talking about earlier.

A number of people do report these past-life experiences. I've taken people through deaths. One past life poet was martyred by starvation in an English prison. He reported the death with powerful, agonal throes that were absolutely convincing. It's interesting, because we don't have a way of talking to someone about what's happening while they're dying. By taking someone through a past life experience, we learn something about the agony of death.

Mishlove: As a therapist and a hypnotist myself, one of the counter-hypotheses that I feel I need to be especially sensitive to is the one that I may be, either through subtle bodily cues or tone of voice or even through telepathy, implanting my ideas in the minds of the people whom I hypnotize. I see that, because I know some therapists who use hypnosis; all of their clients will conform to some model that they have, and another therapist with a different theoretical model seems to get patients who always come up, under hypnosis, with evidence that conforms to their model.

Mack: It's possible that they're somehow reading my mind. I try to be particularly scrupulous about that, and say nothing about anything.

Mishlove: Of course, but as soon as you admit the possibility of telepathy, you can't protect against it.

Mack: Then you get into a whole other matter of how information comes. Is it really about the objective observer listening to the experiencer who is or is not telling "the truth"? Or do we co-create, in a certain sense, our reality? It may not be that they are this repository of facts and I'm this neutral hypnotist or neutral interviewer who's trying to bring out the facts. You and I are creating something that never existed or hasn't happened before, if we're doing our job right. It isn't as if one is simply dealing with a literal nodule of factual experience, and that I'm removing it like a kidney stone. It may be that there's some powerful core of experience, but that I am empowering, in some way, the person to bring that forth.

That could be seen as distortion. It's certainly not leading, because no experiencer or observer I've ever worked with has suggested that I led them. Observers come away shaking their heads, saying, "I know this person. Something powerful happened to this person. I can't explain it, but they wouldn't be making this up. This is not following your lead. It happened." That's how I've gotten some colleagues to join me in this project and be available for referrals.

Mishlove: You mentioned the physical evidence. I think that's very important, because it's one way to counter the argument that this is a *folie à deux*, a folly created by two people. What's the physical evidence that has impressed you the most in the cases you've seen?

Mack: You've put an interesting twist on that. What's impressed *me* the most? It is not the cuts, the scoop marks, [or] the lesions on people's bodies—although those are powerfully corroborative—it's the association with the UFOs. Any theory is going to have to deal with the UFO connection. Frequently, the person experiences the abduction, [and] then they come for help.

I'll give you an example of a case that's in the book. A woman in her mid-twenties comes home from working as a nightclub receptionist. She finds herself compelled to drive in a northeasterly direction from Boston, and ends up in the woods. There's a brilliant light, and she's taken. There's a period of missing time, which is typical, and she experienced a characteristic abduction that she later remembers. She gets home the next morning—she didn't recall seeing a UFO—shocked to see on the television that the major channels reported a UFO moving in exactly the same direction she had been driving. It was independently viewed by the community. The UFO association people just ignore this, with their fancy theories about the psyche. Children as young as two and three years old have had these experiences. How would a sophisticated personality/hallucinatory theory account for a two-year-old boy's abduction experience? I'm thinking of a particular kid who said, "Mommy, don't let the little men take me up into the sky." He woke up with nosebleeds from the procedures that had been done to him. He recoiled when shown a very simple picture of the alien being, included among other much more scary pictures of skeletons and ghosts. He pointed at the alien picture and said that was the one that took him up. If we're going to try to explain it, we have to account for *every* piece of the phenomenon. We can't just take what looks psychological and deal with that. There's other physical evidence though. There are the missing pregnancies and the burned earth outside of the houses where UFOs seem to have landed. I was working with a man who recalled being abducted from his family farm when he was a small boy. A UFO was seen by his father. It left a thirty-foot burn pattern in the field. Nothing would grow there for several years, and the family corroborates that. There *is* physical evidence.

The problem is, for the debunkers, it's not about physical evidence. It's about what I call the politics of perception, or the politics of ontology. Nothing will satisfy them. They say they want an artifact—a piece of a wing off a UFO, something tangible, physical—but if you gave it to them it wouldn't satisfy them; they would simply question the pedigree of it. "Who found it—a little boy in the field? Maybe he made it up. Maybe he told the wrong story." If your mind is already set that things are a certain way, it makes no difference what the physical evidence is.

A science writer in Boston by the name of Chet and I had a very amusing exchange. We'd been going back and forth in the *Boston Globe* about this and he'd been trying to liken all this to medieval witchcraft and all kinds of stuff. I was told, after a rather debunking article in the *Boston Globe*, that I should talk to him. I was reluctant to do it, but I did, and I'm glad I did. It didn't matter what I told him, he knew what he knew. Finally, in exasperation I said, "Chet, look. A UFO could land on the Boston Commons, all the news programs could run footage about it, it could be reported in all the Boston papers, and you still wouldn't believe that it happened; you'd still think it was a hoax." He stopped, silent, but he had the integrity to say, "John, I think you're right." In that kind of situation you're not dealing with matters of physical evidence, you're dealing with a mindset, an ideology, a world view, which has no room for this. One of the reasons I wanted to write the book was to see if I could make some inroads into that world view, to allow that there are other ways of knowing. Perhaps we could reconsider the methodologies of knowledge, the ways we know when we're trying to look at reality beyond this physical world. Maybe Science, with a capital S, is okay for studying things, which are simply in this physical world. As quantum mechanics is showing us, when you're dealing with complex, ambiguous realities, you need something more profound, something like the whole consciousness and expanded ways of knowing.

Mishlove: I sometimes wonder, since some of these debunkers are, in the name of rationality, so clearly irrational, if they themselves aren't unconsciously a part of the very process that we are trying to study, which in some larger sense is the human psyche.

Mack: Indeed. It may be that, for example, the distinction between physical reality and psyche is not as sharp as we like to think. If you ask certain physicists, "What was there before the Big Bang?" They'd say, "That question is not meaningful according to the physical laws that we study." And yet, what are they saying, that the universe appeared out of nothing? Perhaps it appeared out of consciousness, out of the divinity, or the universal mind. Again, that's not physics, that's the boundary, perhaps, between physics and consciousness.

Mishlove: One of the things that you have written about is that this journey has taken you from a very respectable, and largely mainstream, career in psychiatry, to explore the field that is now being called transpersonal psychology, which deals with these kinds of questions and realities.

Mack: Transpersonal psychology really is a fancy word, but all it means is that our consciousness is not the same thing as our bodies and our brains. Our consciousness can separate from our bodies, and we can identify beyond ourselves to connect with realities, with beings, beyond our own skin. This is transpersonal in the sense that the psyches of the abductees, as well as their bodies, can travel into realities that are not supposed to be there.

Mishlove: I thought some of the most interesting cases were the ones—and I'm thinking of one in particular that you wrote about—in which a woman believed herself to be an incarnation of a being who was an alien in a past life, and had been sent here like an advance scout, to be in the Earth plane; to be human.

Mack: There are several cases like that. A very powerful dimension of this phenomenon is what I call the double-identity aspect. When the experiencer gets past the trauma of the reproductive insults, they acknowledge a connection through the eyes, which is a very profound aspect of this. After the bonding occurs through the eye connection they will often experience themselves as aliens, or that they have a whole other identity as an alien. From that perspective they see, frequently in a computer-like vision, all of what we're doing to the earth. They may be involved in human-alien—they being alien—reproductive processes by creating the hybrids. From that perspective they will often feel that that alien self represents the lost souls of human beings. People ask, "Why do these aliens look so humanoid? If they're really something else, why do they look so much like us?" One of the answers may be—and I'm not saying that it's true, but it is one of the areas where I have a fair amount of data—that we both began from a common source. There was a common ground of being before we separated, and humans became densely embodied in the form that we currently are. The aliens remained less embodied but they are part of our being. They are seen as emissaries from the Source, with a capital S, or home, or God, or divinity—again, all these are loaded words, but we have to have some language to talk about what Wittgenstein called the ineffable. One of the many, many dimensions of this phenomenon is the bringing together of our alienated soul self, with the physical, embodied self, to become whole once again. It isn't really two species joining, but a completing of our own identity and wholeness.

Mishlove: I think there's something very profound in that. It reminds me of all of the religious, spiritual, mystical teachings around the world that suggest that ultimately, we are one with the whole universe, and, if that's the case, then truly nothing could really be alien from our deepest nature.

Mack: You wouldn't think that little beings with big black eyes, who appear to be performing nasty, traumatic, rape-like, reproductive invasive procedures would be the source of mystical openings, as you're suggesting, but they are for many individuals. It may be that this is a hard-sell mysticism. If what is occurring, from an evolutionary point of view, is reconnecting us with the ground of being, or Source, then it may be that we can't wait for everyone in the culture to become Buddhist meditators, or discover the Source on their own. It may be that a more intrusive, invasive hit is required—abductions, if you will—to open us up like an intervention, in a sense. It's the crossing over of beings that should stay in the spirit world, coming over into the physical world, because most of us really don't have a way to recognize anything that isn't showing up in the physical world.

Mishlove: John Mack, you've put it quite eloquently. Thanks so much for being with me.

Mack: Thank you for having me, Jeff.

6

UFOs & The Demonic
with
Charles Upton

~

Jeffrey Mishlove: Hello and welcome. I'm Jeffrey Mishlove. Today we will be exploring the relationship between Unidentified Flying Objects (UFOs) and the demonic. My guest is traditionalist philosopher and former Beatnik poet, Charles Upton. His first two books of poetry, *Panic Grass* in 1968 and *Time Raid* in 1969, were published by City Lights in San Francisco, known for publishing the works of the great Beatnik poets. Upton subsequently became engaged in metaphysics and the traditionalist movement and is author of many other books including: *Hammering Hot Iron: A Spiritual Critique of Bly's Iron John*; *Folk Metaphysics: Mystical Meanings in Traditional Folk Songs and Spirituals*; *Cracks in the Great Wall: The UFO Phenomenon and Traditional Metaphysics*; *Knowings in the Arts of Metaphysics, Cosmology, and the Spiritual Path*; *The Science of the Greater Jihad: Essays in Principial Psychology*; *The System of Antichrist: Truth and Falsehood in Postmodernism and the New Age*; *Vectors of the Counter-Initiation: The Course and*

Destiny of Inverted Spirituality, and most recently *The Alien Disclosure Deception: The Metaphysics of Social Engineering.* Charles resides in Lexington, Kentucky.

Welcome, Charles, it's nice to be with you again. Before we get too much further, I want to remind our viewers, they will get a very good sense of your background, both as a poet and as a Traditionalist philosopher, if they watch the first *New Thinking Allowed* video interview, 'From Beatnik to Traditionalist with Charles Upton'.

Charles Upton: Glad to be here and glad to talk about my UFO book, which is on the front burner in my life right now. Unless people get too interested in my Alexander Dugin book [*Dugin Against Dugin: A Traditionalist Critique of the Fourth Political Theory*], given the situation with Ukraine, which seems to be happening, but more later on that.

Mishlove: That will be another very interesting topic. But let's talk about your UFO book now. There are so many threads to it. It has to do with the nature of UFOs, the nature of the demonic, and also I think with the nature of the kinds of deceptive, manipulative activities that are taking place all the time.

Upton: Right, not simply the kind of deceptions that cluster around the UFO phenomenon, but the basic ways that deception is being used for social engineering in so many fields. I would say, to begin with, I am not a ufologist. I am essentially a metaphysician, which means that my ufology is a special application of metaphysics to a particular field or particular phenomenon, which is the UFO phenomenon. I should say, very simplistically, that my book is about a consideration of the ufology of Jacques Vallée—who is, I think, the best of the ufologists, and has been for some time—through the lens of the metaphysics and cosmology of Traditionalist Metaphysician, René Guénon.

What we need to understand about the phenomenon is that we need to first understand the essential nature of being. If we do not understand that, UFO encounters will be continuously anomalous and strange events that people pursue one by one, trying to figure them out. Are they extraterrestrial astronauts, are they hoaxes, or are they interdimensional beings? What is an interdimensional being? People go down different rabbit holes, all of which have a certain amount of truth, but they do not have a unified vision of how all these things relate.

Jacques Vallée essentially came up with three aspects of the UFO phenomenon, and he went pretty deeply into all of them. One of them is the physical evidence. Are these things real in that sense? Apparently so. They appear on radar, they leave physical traces, and there are certainly physical effects on people who claim to be abducted. All of this is documented. That's one set of data. The other is, they are beings who are, apparently, psychic and paranormal and they deeply affect our psyches. They're partially material, translucent and appear and disappear out of nowhere. Sometimes the UFO aliens walk through the walls into your bedroom then into dreams. So there is all of that. Then the third aspect of their strangeness is the human deception activities, as I like to say, of the *Mission Impossible* variety—for anybody who remembers that program— clustered around the event. It's very hard for people to put these three points together. How can it be all three? In other words, when I talk about the deception aspect of the phenomenon, people say, "Are you saying that the UFOs are all hoaxes?" No, I'm not. If you say they're psychic, then people say, "Well, then they could not be astronauts." You say they are astronauts, and they say, "Well, how can they affect you psychically?" People go around in circles. Whereas from a standpoint of traditional metaphysics, you can see that there is a base phenomenon. It's a certain type; always reported and it emanates from a particular level on the hierarchy of being.

Traditional metaphysics includes, among other things, three aspects. One is ontology, the science of being and of hierarchy. It is the hierarchy of being with levels that show us how the universe is constructed. This can be found, in one way or another, in almost every sacred tradition. You can find things in Lakota myth that are like Thomas Aquinas, if you know how to read the symbols and have read the doctrines. There is a great unanimity in the sense of how being *is*. Then a second one, that we're talking about today, is demonology, or how the hierarchy of being can be subverted or attempt to be subverted in particular instances. The third is eschatology, the science of apocalypse, because I believe that the UFO phenomenon, at this point in history, is related to our being in these latter days.

All of this goes back to traditional metaphysics. If you have a clear understanding of that discipline, UFOs are not a mystery. You can't reach certainty as to what they are in every instance. There may be some that are hoaxes and some that are delusions. There may be some which are tests of secret human technology that are taking place under the cover of the UFO idea. "Well, these must be from another planet!" But if there wasn't a basic phenomenon, then hoaxes would be pointless and those clandestine tests of arcane technology? There would be no way to cover them up. Unless there are UFO phenomena, you cannot use it to cover up other phenomena.

I think what UFOs are has always been known, in general terms, by those who understand the nature of being. In some cases, there were whole societies who had a general idea of what these things were. In other cases it was only small groups of philosophers. This is nothing new. We know what these are.

Mishlove: You are referring in particular to the metaphysics of René Guénon. In our previous interview, we talked a lot about your background in traditionalist thinking and philosophy, your relationship to Frithjof Schuon and to our mutual friend, Huston Smith. We haven't talked about René Guénon, really, to any extent, so maybe you could fill our viewers in, a little bit, about his background.

Upton: He was a French philosopher and metaphysician, who operated in the 20th century and died in 1951. Like people in the 1960s onward, he researched all of the occult groups that he could find in France, between the two wars, maybe a bit before. He was connected with the Martinists, the Neo-Gnostics, and the Theosophical Society. He was very hot to find the mystical, the occult, or metaphysical secrets. He didn't entirely come out of Freemasonry, but he came out of this world saying this stuff is not just crazy, it's subversive. There is a lot of evil going on here.

At the same time, he was studying the traditional doctrines of the world religions such as Taoism, but particularly Vedanta. He wrote a couple of wonderful books: one was a classic called *Man and His Becoming According to the Vedanta*. He was studying the esoteric or inner meanings of the world's religions. He came to the conclusion that this kind of knowledge is on an infinitely higher and more wholesome level than the knowledge of the general esotericist occultist groups, some of whom are overt Satanists. There is esoteric knowledge. However, it wouldn't be found in this stew of cults in France and Europe during the time Guénon was investigating them.

Two of his first books were exposés of spiritualism and the Theosophical Society. They were exposés like we have nowadays and were very well done. He wrote many books on pure metaphysics, and on the metaphysical exegesis of poetry, myth and symbolism. His concluding masterpiece was, *The Reign of Quantity and the Signs of the Times*, essentially his take on eschatology. He believed that we're coming to the end of this *manvantara*, the Hindu term for a cycle of manifestation. This is very much like the lore of Christianity and Islam: that we are now in the latter days, or the last days of the Kali Yuga, in Hindu terms. Guénon wrote a very abstract but very powerful book on, more or less, the science of Apocalypse describing how the final phases of this cycle will work out, and why it's happening, metaphysically. His brilliant thing was to take the cycle of *manvantara* and express it in Aristotelian-Thomistic terms. In western terms, the four yugas can be described as the golden age, the silver age, the bronze age, and the iron age, each darker and shorter than the one before, then a return to a golden age for the next cycle.

He said the *manvantara* cycle is coming from a condition of essence or form, and descending, through various stages, from the essential pole to the substantial pole. The substantial pole is matter, considered to be self-sufficient without the spirit but it's extremely chaotic, and virtually without form. It cannot be completely without form, otherwise it wouldn't exist. In the early ages of the cycle, qualities and form are paramount, time is slower, space is dominant, [and] we get closer to a sense of eternity. In the latter days of the cycle, everything is whooshing past like a bat out of hell, and form is breaking, becoming chaotic. This is perfectly descriptive of what is happening now.

What Guénon said was, late in the cycle, a figure will appear in the energy wall that some call the etheric wall noted in the Qur'an. This figure is called Dhu al-Qarnayn, which means "two-horned" but we don't know who he is. Is it Alexander the Great? It's a myth that people have disputed for centuries. Dhu al-Qarnayn goes to the extremities of the world, from East to West, and finds the hordes of Gog and Magog are breaking through. He creates this huge iron wall to keep them out but Guénon said that wall is starting to break down and letting in intrapsychic forces, which is the energy wall between the material plane and the subtle plane. We can see that clearly, especially with the development of LSD, nuclear weapons, and electronic technology. This world is not as solid as it used to be. It's becoming volatilized, and very dark intrapsychic forces are breaking through from below, through the cracks in this great wall.

Guénon wrote that this leak is what is going to happen first, because when the great wall is solid, and when nothing is breaking through from either below or above, it is like 19th century materialism. Even in science fiction movies of the 20th century, someone would say, "This cannot be happening; this is the 20th century!" Well, I'm sorry, but now we're in the 21st century, and this stuff is breaking through. This is the anti-tradition movement, according to Guénon, which is materialism to counter-tradition, a perversion of spiritual truth, very often a very conscious perversion of it. This is where we are now.

There will be more cracks appearing in an upward direction in the wall. Through these cracks will come, let us say, the Messiah, in which all traditions have a different aspect, different names for the Messiah. In Christianity, it is the Christ of the Parousia. He is named the Messiah in Judaism. In Islam, he is the Mahdi, and the Mahdi is, more properly, the herald of the Messiah, the prophet Jesus, and he will slay the Antichrist. In Hinduism, he is the Kalki Avatara, who will initiate the new age, the new cycle of manifestation. In Buddhism, it's Maitreya. You will find this figure throughout all the world's religions.

When the cracks start to open in an upward direction, first there will be a great angelic manifestation, here now, if you can sense it. Finally, things are not going to be allowed to get ultimately dark. Lastly, the human form will not be totally perverted. The world, as we know it, may not survive. This does not mean that evil will triumph, by any means. Just speaking psycho-physically, the crack in the upward direction is the *brahmarandhra*, the point at the crown of the skull, understood in yoga as a point of opening to higher states of consciousness. The Hopis have the same thing. They say always keep the door in the top of your head open. Keep listening through that door because that is where guidance comes from. That is the opening in the upward direction. So, this is the framework of eschatology that I am essentially working through when speaking of UFOs. It is mostly from Guénon, but of course, Guénon draws on many, many different traditions. This is not his personal invention.

Mishlove: I suppose it is fair to point out that, among traditionalists, there are diverging points of view on many of the finer points here. You mentioned you were very influenced by Frithjof Schuon, who, as I recall from our previous conversation, had some falling out with Guénon.

Upton: Schuon wanted to be the authority. He took much from Guénon. Schuon had some legitimate critiques of Guénon that were valid. Guénon said the Catholic Church had lost its inner-dimension, completely, one of the reasons why he spent so much time with Freemasonry. He was trying to find or invent or create an esoteric inner-dimension that could take its place, in the Catholic Church, because he thought the Church had lost it. The Church might have lost, largely, an understanding of its treasures, but Schuon came forward announcing Guénon was wrong. Schuon believed the initiatory inner dimension of the Catholic Church is its sacraments, i.e. the initiatory rites: baptism, confirmation, and Holy Eucharist. Essentially, Dionysius the pseudo-Areopagite, early Christian father, had exactly the same initiatory sense of Christianity in his book, the *Ecclesiastical Hierarchy [The Celestial Hierarchy]*.

They differed legitimately. Guénon was certainly more sophisticated in understanding the darkness of the world and what was going on, while Schuon largely, although not entirely, ignored it. Schuon was right on this point, in my opinion Guénon did not really understand Catholic or Christian initiation. In fact, Guénon did not understand or know much about hesychast, a more or less initiatory spiritual way within Eastern Orthodoxy. It is close-informed to Sufism and almost, strangely enough, identical. The closer people or religions are to each other, the more they fight. It is very, very similar. Schuon did not know much about the parallel. But then Schuon had his own problems. He was initiated in a Sufi order, a legitimate Sufi order, of the Alawiyya under Sheikh Ahmad al-Alawi. Then he ran off and did his own order, without real authorization, because he had visions of the Virgin Mary. He did some very interesting things, wrote interesting books, said very enlightening and helpful things, particularly for our time. But his group became, well—he had one of the classic guru meltdowns, that we have seen so many of. He conducted rituals of sacred nudity and things like this. If you want to make sure something is going to go wrong, just do that. Particularly if you say you are a Muslim and call yourself a Sufi master, and then you do that. Doesn't work. A lot of enlightenment and a lot of wisdom came out of Schuon, but you really have to pick and choose, and you do have to criticize where he went wrong.

Mishlove: With regard to the whole UFO circus that we seem to be immersed in, it strikes me that in some ways it's not so different from how you have described the Traditionalist movement. There are many different threads. There are some people I've talked to who consider themselves contactees. They describe their experience as almost entirely, if not entirely, angelic, with the beings having nothing but positive hopes and wishes for humanity. I know in your work you focus on the demonic side.

Upton: I would not say that those experiences are necessarily false. I am saying that UFOs exhibit the phenomenology of the beings known as the djinn, who are subtle material beings, but not properly spiritual as angels are. It may be that angels can only become convincing to people, nowadays, by presenting themselves as aliens, for all I know. What I want to say is, that there is so much darkness in that world. According to the Qur'an, some of the djinn are Muslims. Some of the djinn are positive and good. They worship Allah. They follow the Qur'an, yet others are not. Generally speaking, the djinn bend to a demonic direction.

I am going to read you a quote from John Mack who was a psychiatrist and a Pulitzer Prize-winning author who wrote something on T.E. Lawrence, Lawrence of Arabia. He became one of the few psychiatrists who studied and treated people abducted by aliens. Mack had a very positive view of [aliens]. He said, "These beings are here to teach us," and he was pro-alien.

Yet, this is his description after perhaps 100 people he treated: "John E. Mack … recounts nearly 100 cases of human abductions by aliens, many of whose victims he personally treated, and lists among the effects on them of such unfortunate encounters: 'physical and psychological scars of their experience, ranging from nightmares and anxiety to chronic nervous agitation, depression, even psychosis, to actual physical scars, puncture and incision marks, scrapes, burns, and sores.' He informs us that the alien abductors routinely subject their victims to terrifying and humiliating medical-like procedures. They also voyeuristically view them performing sexual intercourse or themselves have intercourse with them. He speaks of broken marriages, and alienation of affection between parents and children, as among the more common aftereffects and says that negative physical and psychological effects persist, even in cases where spontaneous healing of chronic or incurable diseases occurs."

He was pro-alien. He thought this was all good. To me, that is a description of something I never want to have happen to me. It is perfectly in line with what is known in various religious traditions—Eastern Orthodox Christianity, and Catholic exorcism—about what demons are and how they appear, and their effects. Like I often say, not every fish in shark-infested waters is a shark. That does not mean it's safe to swim in shark-infested waters. There are innumerable different beings on the subtle psychic plane, some of whom are helpful. You cannot say that a nature spirit, the spirit of a beautiful oak tree out in the woods, the subtle deva or spirit of that tree, is evil. That is not evil. They are doing their job keeping the forest growing. This is a very good thing. But generally speaking, there is much evil involved when tapping into the never when.

The other thing is that I believe that elements of the military-industrial-intelligence complex, starting basically after World War II, looked and said, "We cannot figure out what these beings are." They started as the foo fighters in World War II, noticed by the bomber crews flying on bomb runs to Germany. Orbs would follow their planes. Then, right after World War II, there is Roswell and the Kenneth Arnold sightings. I believe the powers that be said, "We can't figure out what these are; we cannot control them. But, guess what? We can use them. We can craft a myth surrounding the UFO phenomenon that we will slowly project into society so that whenever one of these events happens, as a sighting or an abduction, they will seem to confirm the myth. This is the way we will control how people think about it."

The problem with this supposition is that myth is directly anti-religious. There is a quote by William Sims Bainbridge, co-director of Cyber-Human Systems at the National Science Foundation, senior fellow of the Institute for Ethics and Emerging Technologies, and one of our most prominent transhumanists. He wrote this forty years ago, but he is still in those positions now, or at least at the National Science Foundation.

He said, "These flying saucer cults are all quite insignificant, but one like them could well rise to prominence in a future decade. We need several really aggressive, attractive space religions meeting the emotional needs of different segments of our population, driving traditional religions and retrograde cults from the field." Now, here the UFO myth is being openly presented as the enemy of every traditional religion on earth. Judaism, Christianity, Islam, Hinduism, Buddhism, all of them, all are described as retrograde cults.

The problem with the UFO myth, as it has been crafted, is that one of its major dogmas denies that the human race was created by God. Instead, we were created by the UFO aliens through genetic engineering. We are their lab rats. Therefore, any concept of human dignity is out the window, and there is an overt attack on religion. Whenever Stephen Greer mentions the word religion, he just boils over with snake venom. "Religious nuts, religious fanatics." He hates religions. That hatred has got to have a reason for it. To the degree that we see fulminating hatred of the religions, we are witnessing something demonic.

I think this is very much supported by John Mack's description of the basic diagnoses in the 100 cases of UFO alien abductions he describes. I am not saying that a positive event cannot come out of the paranormal. They do all the time. Angels come out of the paranormal. It may be that people do not believe in angels. "What is an angel? Some say, it is stupid, a girly type with wings. I don't want to see that." I do not know how these things operate. It is very imponderable. People could have had positive experiences, but we must not ignore the great preponderance of terribly negative influences coming from the UFO phenomenon. And the way the powers-that-be are taking hold of this darkness, to use it to mold our consciousness, and change our society from one that has been basically Christian and democratic to Luciferian and transhumanistic. This is what is going on now.

Mishlove: Back to traditionalist metaphysics. I think it would be fair to say that the metaphysical cosmology that you're subscribing to, and that you attribute to people like Guénon and Frithjof Schuon, is one in which there is a vast hierarchy of beings. They range from God, ultimately, at the top, and the Heavenly Host or angels, and on to nature spirits and devas. Then below that, there is a demonic order. Mostly it features a sort of satanic figure, an antichrist, or a being almost the equivalent of God, but not quite, because it must have been a creation of God at its beginning.

Upton: What I ask is, "Do you believe that Satan exists as an individual being?" Big question. My response is partly tongue-in-cheek, "Well, he would like to exist, but he does not have what it takes." What is the shadow of something? It would not exist without the light, without the object that the light is shining on, to cast a shadow. The shadow is real, in a sense, but in another sense, it is not real. It's real in the sense that it has effects. If you fall into the shadow, you cannot see. You will stumble over something and hurt yourself, at the very least.

Evil is essentially a privation. Thomas Aquinas called it, a *privatio boni*, a privation of the good and of the real. It is a hole in the being with a great effect. If you walk along and fall into a hole, you may die. The power of that hole is not because it has positive being, but because it is a privation, an emptiness. It is not an emptiness in the Buddhist sense, but something beyond all determinations. It acts as a vampire on more integrated levels of being. That is one of the things universal manifestation makes necessary, and one of its possibilities. All possibilities must be manifested in the course of the cycle.

Mishlove: My own sense of the demonic is that the first place one should look for is within oneself. I have a sense that a lot of the greatest evil that has been done on this planet was done in the name of fighting evil. It becomes what the Jungians call a projection. That is the great danger of trying to point out the demonic somewhere outside of oneself.

Upton: It is inside oneself, too. If you want to talk about the Antichrist, I consider the Antichrist to be the manifestation of the collective ego of humanity. Ego, not in the sense of the conscious personality that can make decisions, but in the negative sense. It is that which stands in the way of spiritual realization. The ego—egotism—which can be defined as obsessive self-definition instead of letting God define you, or being willing to be who God knows you to be. You say, "No, I am going to invent my own self. Forget it. I don't need you." You then obsessively try to figure out who you are in an effort to make yourself better or justify yourself.

The collective ego of humanity will manifest and is manifesting as the Antichrist, because we are getting near the end of the cycle. There are many ways that all this could end, and we see this ending wherever we look, which produces a profound universal fear. When people are in a state of fear, they do one thing or another: say, "All right, God, thy will be done. What is to be will be. All is in the hands of God. Whatever happens, if I maintain my faith in God, and that the universe is not ultimately wrong, then something good, perhaps inconceivable to me now, will come out of this." Or you can decide to not think about this, and do anything not to let this happen.

Weapons of mass distraction come in because of the universal fear. You do not have to worry about nuclear war, because you can go into the metaverse where you can have anything you want, any fantasy you want, that can be three-dimensionally manifested through virtual reality goggles. If this really takes hold it is going to be phenomenally destructive to the human soul and human society.

It's like the stages of death that Elisabeth Kübler-Ross talked about in her book *On Death and Dying.* An entire society can go through those stages of death. There is one point where we might say, "If we pool all our egos into one big ego, that will save us." In a certain sense, because we are afraid, we are looking for a materialistic Antichrist who will magically make all the consequences of our actions evaporate, without our having to live them out. Whatever it is that promises to do this is an aspect of a system of Antichrist. There may be, at one point, an actual human figure who is the center of that, or it could be just a system, but it is the tendency.

There is a point in which forces of darkness can come in and make promises to solve the things you fear most. There was a Netflix original series, which I analyzed in my book, called *Top Secret UFO Projects Declassified*, which brings together that whole UFO myth, as crafted. One of the things said in the program is, "When the UFO aliens come, they will solve our environmental problems. They will end war and economic disparities." These are the promises being made and something we are to expect from beings who do all those terrible things to human beings that John Mack described. We're supposed to put our hope in them, because if we are afraid enough, we will put our hope in anything. It's a bit like Stockholm Syndrome.

Mishlove: Let's define that for readers who may not know about Stockholm Syndrome.

Upton: I forgot the incident that it came from, but there were some people who were kidnapped by terrorists, and they began to develop a great love and trust in the people who had kidnapped them. The brainwashing technique used is when torture is alternated with relief and regret on the part of the torturer. They will say to the prisoner, "Look, we didn't really want to do this. I do not enjoy this, okay? It's just we have to go through this because we have the thing that we are doing. But really, I have no personal animosity with you and I kind of like you." And the prisoner responds, "Oh yeah, yeah, I like you too, man. Thanks a lot." The relief drives people crazy and they misinterpret relief from torture as the torturer offering friendship.

Mishlove: I was living in Berkeley during the Patty Hearst kidnapping by the Symbionese Liberation Army. Here she was, a wealthy heiress, who ended up joining a group of terrorists after she had been kidnapped.

Upton: We don't know the whole Patty Hearst story. Who knows what was going on? If the way it was presented to us is true, then it is a perfect example of Stockholm Syndrome.

Mishlove: It strikes me, Charles, with regard to UFOs and the idea that there is some manipulation going on behind the scenes—I think what you are saying is UFOs are essentially paranormal, largely demonic—that this fact is being used by some very powerful, "... powers-that-be ... ," for their own purposes. It strikes me that we live in a largely pluralistic society where there are dozens of different groups. And all are pushing their own agendas. I believe, at the end of the day, there are very few real "powers" that are capable of influencing society to move in one direction.

Upton: If society was influenced to move in a certain direction to such a degree that the change was universal, all-pervading and people did not notice, because it was the status quo, they would say exactly what you said. In my book, you will see a lot of the history of the social engineering project since World War II that went into crafting the UFO myth. The number of Central Intelligence Agency (CIA) people involved in and on the boards of UFO groups is phenomenal (e.g. To The Stars Academy). The CIA has been doing social engineering ever since MK-ULTRA, which probably is still going on in some way or another, so this should not come as a surprise to anyone. Do you remember in 1962 General Douglas MacArthur's speech?

Mishlove: Yes, I recall that.

Upton: In a speech to the cadets at West Point on May 12, 1962, he says, "We deal now not with the things of this world alone, but with the illimitable distances and as yet unfathomed mysteries of the universe, of ultimate conflict between a united human race and the sinister forces of some other planetary galaxy, of such dreams and fantasies as to make life the most exciting of all times. And through all this welter of change and development, your mission remains fixed, determined, inviolable. It is to win our wars." When he said this in 1962, it created the lie that the US government was only trying to debunk UFOs for the past seventy years. A double message creates cognitive dissonance in the population, making them highly susceptible to suggestion and manipulation.

Mishlove: This, I think, is one of the most profound ideas in your book. We are getting contradictory messages like this, sometimes referred to as a double blind, and there is a theory that this is what produces schizophrenia.

Upton: Yes, exactly. In my book I am proposing that these techniques, which I call "unconscious contradiction" and "deferred closure", are experimental methods of creating schizophrenia. Wouldn't MK-ULTRA be very interested in these techniques? It's hard to admit we are being manipulated. People do not have a comprehensive enough view of things, only seeing one part of it, and become obsessed. Conspiracy theories are not about terrible things going on that we *don't* know about, or are not fully understood. The paranoid part comes in when the person says, "No, I understand it. I got the whole thing. It's this!" referring to just one piece of the issue. We have so many examples of people who have taken an element of the truth and become obsessed by it, until it becomes absurd and ridiculous. This puts the whole enterprise of investigating hidden social and psychological forces in a bad light, because of the obsessions of unbalanced people.

But if we were to have a fuller concept of things, and I think the first step is to have some sense of metaphysical reality, then I think it is possible to investigate, without reaching premature closure, what paranoia is. The schizophrenic has too much information he tries to make sense of because the human mind needs this. We need to have some belief system to say, "What is reality?" A premature closure is made on this flood of data by abnormal means, and that is what a paranoid delusional system is. It's the closure that is the problem. I have made closures myself, I guess, but we will see who turns up crazy. Not in this world, probably.

Mishlove: It will be interesting if we could stick around long enough to see how the final act plays out. The question that I have at this point is, to what extent is this schizophrenic reality, and reality does seem to be very schizophrenic, to what extent is it the result of deliberate manipulation by the powers-that-be, and to what extent is it the natural product of a pluralistic universe?

Upton: The second aspect of this is the natural product of the disorganization of things and the loss of form at the end of a cycle, and the descent of the *manvantara* into the substantial pole. This is materialistic chaos, much like the Heisenberg indeterminacy. René Guénon said, "... the degeneration of the cosmic environment happens inevitably in the course of a cycle." What this does is bring negative possibilities forward, but it does not actualize them. Human groups are required to actualize the possibilities.

There were times when the dark things being done to us now could not have been done, because then we were closer to social cohesion, psychological balance, and a sense of spiritual reality. Now there is a great deal of scope for it to occur. There are various groups that come forward to say, "Ah, now the human race is weak enough. We can do our thing." I like to say the devil is an opportunistic infection of the psychic immune system. When the sense of psychic integrity becomes weakened, then all sorts of forces from without can invade. This is the relationship between the demonic and what is going on in our souls. When we are in a state where the demonic can affect us, can pervert our will, our affections, and our intelligence, we have been damaged. Either by our own actions or by trauma, by whatever may have happened to us in life, we become weakened to a point where outer forces can affect us.

Mishlove: Do you feel for yourself, in particular, or for other people that this means you have lost control of your life?

Upton: Control of my life? The one who has my life in his hands is God. My control is only provisional, at best. Things can go wrong. You can get sick, lose your money, or suffer from a collective disaster. Do we ever have control of our lives in a real sense? We have as much as we can put together. I have found that I have no shape or stability in my life unless I say to God, "Thy will be done." Then His will operates so things start to make sense and start to go in a coherent direction. Whereas if I say, "You know what I would like to do; I think I need more of this…" then things start to go to hell. It may simply be that I have not had the resources some people have to maintain the illusion of self-determination. I've had to recognize my weaknesses, my inadequacies, my psychological imbalances, and circumstantial deficiencies. This is one of the things that brings you closer to God. You have to keep praying or things go to hell.

Mishlove: It sounds as if you are saying that there is some sort of a demonic force that manifests itself paranormally that has struck up, consciously or unconsciously, an alliance with various powers- that-be.

Upton: I would not say it is absolutely certain, but I would certainly say many things may suggest the premise. Do you know Jack Parsons?

Mishlove: The co-founder of the Jet Propulsion Lab.

Upton: And of the Aerojet Corporation. He was an early rocket scientist who has a crater named after him on the dark side of the moon. He presented early plans for the Pentagon building, and was very much integrated within the powers-that-be. The thing is, he was a pagan magician who did magical invocations at his rocket launchings. He was a fellow student along with L. Ron Hubbard—the founder of Scientology—of black magician Aleister Crowley, who was not only a black magician but [also] a member of British intelligence.

They gathered at the Agape Lodge in Los Angeles. Parsons said, "My purpose in life is to destroy Christianity." I found on YouTube an old film of him doing what he called the Babalon Workings, where he was invoking this being named Babalon. Parsons had something he described as an electronic ouija board. In the background, you could hear a small audience, and the filmmaker, asking, "What are you doing here?" "Oh, you see—he said—this is how we invoke demons." It was Babalon, a female demon that he worked with.

We know that UFOs have an effect on electronics. When a UFO flies over a car, the engine dies. It is understandable that Parsons would create some box with an electromagnetic field where a demon could stick his finger in and do a Ouija board communication. So he is doing demonic invocation, saying, "I'm here to destroy Christianity," and he is the founder of JPL. So you think that there is no coming together of the powers-that-be, in a worldly sense, and the demonic? Certainly there is. I just do not know how universal it is, whether he was an odd bird and no one else did it. I think some other people did it too—are doing it—but I can't prove that so I am going to leave that as a question.

Mishlove: It gets tricky. It gets very subtle because I think you would agree that even in Christianity, which has done a lot of good in the world, that it's not immune from what one might call demonic infestation within the church itself.

Upton: The Catholic Church now is officially pro-alien. Corrado Balducci, who was the exorcist for the Diocese of Rome, said that the UFO aliens are not demons, nor examples of spirit attachment. He used a term from spiritualism, not from Catholicism, but what he meant was, they are not a demonic possession. He said, "When they come, we would baptize them. Maybe they can baptize us."

A very positive view of the aliens, which is in line with Pope Francis' statement that was on the Vatican website for years where he says in an interview with the Vatican Radio, "Guess what? God does not exist." He says, "You are shocked? God does not exist? So what? God does not exist. We don't need God. We have the three persons of the Blessed Trinity. We've got them. So what is this God, pray? It does not exist." In other words, he denies the central dogma of the Catholic Church, the Nicene Creed: *Credo in unum Deum*, "I believe in one God." He reduces the Christian Trinity to a trio of pagan gods, or polytheism, and this is no longer Christianity at all. Father Malachi Martin believed that the Vatican had been dedicated to Lucifer in a particular ritual that happened at one point. What is coming from the Catholic Church leadership is quite sinister.

Mishlove: You don't have to only look at the present. You can go back to medieval times and see all kinds of atrocities.

Upton: That was corruption and there has always been corruption. The Renaissance popes such as the Medicis owned whorehouses where they got the proceeds. They were the pimps that kept the phenomenon out of polite society. This is not what you would hope to see when looking at the Catholic Church, but there has been corruption all along. Only recently has there been total subversion; total heresy; total apostasy.

Mishlove: There was the Inquisition. There was the burning of witches. Those things are not the result of corruption.

Upton: That was evil. That was corrupt. But it was not apostate. Apostate is going to go over to the heretics rather than burn them. That is a different thing.

Mishlove: One can look at pagan society, pretty much wiped out by the Church, and see that it did have some positive elements.

Upton: Of course, it had many positive elements. The problem with pagan society is, it got old. There must have been a revelation that the Greco-Roman paganism came from. It may have been from the Orphic tradition, and certainly there was a lot absorbed from Egypt, where there was a very high religious and spiritual understanding. Paganism just got old. People in the mystery cults, perhaps—we don't know much about it—or the Neo-Platonists could hark back to a much higher potential than paganism. But the idea of Zeus, as the personification of the one, as the father of gods and men, is way different from Zeus, one of the many gods, the first among equals, who has rivalry with other gods, has problems with his wife, then commits adultery. Obviously, the conception of the divine degenerated over vast eons. Whenever this happens, God sends a new revelation.

Christianity did not wipe out paganism; it supplanted and sometimes suppressed it. Other times, the pagans really wanted something new, because they were tired of the greatest whorehouse in the world being the Temple of Diana [Artemis] in Ephesus, and everyone being afraid of magic. I went to Bath once, in England—which was the location of a Roman bath—and I saw this pile of little pottery shards. People would write curses against their enemies on these pieces of pottery and throw them into the bath as offerings to the goddess Solovar, a local goddess, who was syncretized with a Roman goddess. Everybody was superstitious. It was a very, very sad world in late antiquity so a lot of the pagans accepted Christianity with open arms.

In other cases, the Christians persecuted the pagans and the Platonic academies were closed so they went to Persia to survive.

The Greco-Roman world was falling apart and Christianity was able to have some effect on civilizing the barbarians making the Europe that is only now falling apart for almost 2,000 years. There is always evil involved in religions because there is evil involved in this world, and in the human soul. I make a clear distinction between corruption and evil, and apostasy and a conscious turn against God. This is a different level, and is fairly recent in the Catholic Church.

Mishlove: We have writers like the great Swiss psychiatrist, Carl Jung—whom I know you take issue with—who wrote about flying saucers as the birth of a new religion. He suggests that the saucer shape, the circle, is a symbol of wholeness, that there might be some positive rejuvenation in society coming from this.

Upton: Let's see what happens. There are a lot of weird, misshapen things, like the dark knight satellite that was supposed to change shape. Certainly, not all UFOs are flying saucers, but that is a classic shape. What does it mean that it has radial symmetry unlike living beings or craft in this world? That is an interesting point. What you have to see is the general drift of it. I do not necessarily go along with what Jung is saying.

Mishlove: We can have a whole other conversation about your critique of Jung.

Upton: Jung was very important in my development and I think he had a lot of very deep perceptions. There is an element where Jung believed in God, but did not accept God, as a part of the system. Essentially, Jung's basic reality was collective subjectivity, the collective unconscious, or the imprints of past experiences on earlier phases of humanity. That is all there, but that is not God, if you say that's basic reality. Individuation is interesting. Some of the things he said about the self-archetype are very close to what the Sufis say about *al-Qalb* or the spiritual heart. There is a confluence there that you can learn from it, certainly. There are certain Jungians I am very glad existed, like Marie-Louis von Franz.

My only problem with her is her Jungianism. She was so smart and had so many perceptive things to say, like about natural justice. You may think you have escaped the long arm of the law, but the furies and natural justice will get you. Two of the deepest things Jung said: whatever is repressed is projected. Now you can go to town with that; it is brilliant. The other one is that you are going to individuate one way or the other. If you do it consciously, then wonderful. If you cooperate with the process, you can really become self-actualized in a wonderful way. Whereas, if not, it is going to happen anyway but it will happen in an inverted and ironic way. You will end up becoming just what you were destined to be, you poor bastard. In neither case can you avoid the process. I think that is very deep.

Mishlove: That sounds like an example of von Franz's natural justice.

Upton: Yes, it is. I am probably seeing this through von Franz's eyes.

Mishlove: Wouldn't you also say, Charles, that the present situation, the UFO disclosure deception that you write about is also an example of natural justice?

Upton: Yes. I wrote something recently saying this is the time when everyone will have to reveal exactly the idols they worship. No one can hide them anymore. They will have to live out the inevitable consequences of that worship. There is no more time to say maybe it will go some other way. That is natural or divine justice, not legal justice.

Mishlove: Charles Upton, we could continue this conversation for a long time, I'm sure. It is delightful to talk to you. It's really eye opening. I appreciate the fact that you are coming from this position. You know where you are coming from, and that gives a lot of strength to your arguments. Even if I disagree, I enjoy the conversation very much. I am looking forward to similar conversations with you in the future.

Upton: Yes, so am I. I enjoy talking with you, too. I'm glad you challenge me as much as you do. I am glad you do not challenge me more than you do.

Mishlove: Charles, thank you very much for being with me today.

Upton: Glad to be here, and I look forward to more of the same.

7

A New Vision of the Unexplained: Part 1
with
Whitley Strieber

~

Jeffrey Mishlove: Our topic today is a new vision of the unexplained. With me is Whitley Strieber, author of more than forty books, including many well-known horror and science fiction novels, such as *Wolfen*. There are also a number of bestselling non-fiction books including *Communion: A True Story, Breakthrough: The Next Step, Solving the Communion Enigma: What is to Come, The Key: A True Encounter, The Secret School: Preparation for Contact, Transformation: The Breakthrough*. He is also co-author with Anne Strieber of *The Communion Letters: The Truth is Out There for Those Who Dare to Read It*, and *The Afterlife Revolution*. He is co-author with Professor Jeffrey Kripal of *The Supernatural: A New Vision of the Unexplained*, which will be the focus of today's interview. That book is really a summary and analysis of his previous nonfiction books. Also, he wrote the foreword for Jacques Vallées' book *Dimensions: A Casebook of Alien Contact*.

Welcome, Whitley. It's a pleasure to be with you. I've been looking forward to interviewing you for a long time.

Whitley Strieber: Me too, Jeffrey. We've had plenty of trouble getting this scheduled, so I'm very glad to be here.

Mishlove: We're going to be talking about the book, *The Supernatural*, that you co-authored with Jeffrey Kripal. It strikes me, as I look at your portion of that book, that it's basically a summary of your nonfiction work over the last 30 years.

Strieber: Yes, it's exactly that. It's a summation of a very extraordinary life experience, one that I either was intended for or that I happened into. I'm not really sure which. But, it has been a remarkable life and it still is. If anything, more is going on now than has ever gone on in my life before. It's quite incredible.

Mishlove: One of the themes that really struck me as I look back on your work is that you have been endeavoring, quite consistently, to attract the attention of the scholarly community, the scientific community and the world at large. Your fundamental claim is that this is a phenomenon that you don't want to necessarily label because there are many possible labels, but whatever it is, it's real and it deserves serious attention.

Strieber: I have been trying to do that and have actually had some success with it or there wouldn't be Jeffrey Kripal as a co-author. He's a very distinguished scholar. I've also had some success in the scientific community as well. But there I'm rather limited in that the only evidence I have possession of, and science needs evidence to work with, is implanted in my ear and I don't want them taken out. I've learned how to use this thing and I wouldn't break it for the world.

Mishlove: Let's start there then. It's a good entryway. I know you describe in the book of having a very distinct memory, of I think, two individuals, they looked human, as I recall.

Strieber: They did.

Mishlove: Basically, they inserted this object, which remains in, I gather, in the earlobe.

Strieber: It's right here, in the midpoint of my left ear. It happened in May of 1989. In one of my books it says May of 1994, but that's a typographical error from the publisher. I was awake but I had just turned out the light, getting ready to go to sleep. I think I had just dozed off and then I heard gravel crunching in the driveway under the bedroom windows; we had a gravel driveway there. It was the sound of tires on the gravel but no headlights shown. We had a big heavy gate that you couldn't get through at night. Plus, no one who shows up at your house in the middle of the night without headlights, getting past a heavy locked gate, is going to be good news. That was very clear at once. As I became aware of this I sat up in bed and heard a voice in the backyard say very clearly, "Condition red."

At that moment I saw a man and a woman standing in the doorway—the bedroom had a doorway at the end that led into a corridor. The woman was in front, the man behind. They immediately rushed forward. At first when I heard the gravel, I was trying to turn on a bank of floodlights situated all around the house. But after I heard the voice and saw the people I started to go for the shotgun under my bed instead. I was aware that the LEDs on the alarm system were still red. In other words, the alarm system had not been turned off. They got to the bedside. What I then remember is I was lying on my right side, facing my wife who was on the other side of the bed, and someone was pressing down on the left side of my head, on this ear, it felt like with their hand, or something. The woman was speaking very soothingly to me. Then it ended.

There was a flash of light and a great deal of crashing in the woods, as if someone was running. I leaped out of bed, grabbed the pistol from the bedside table. I lived in a virtual armory in those days. I began running through the house because the alarm system was armed but these people had been there.

There was no question whatsoever in my mind about it. I went through the attic, basement, everywhere. There was not a single breach at all. I went back to sitting on the bedside thinking, was this some kind of incredibly bizarre dream? What am I actually capable of here? I finally lay down and went into an uneasy half sleep for the rest of the night.

In the morning I told Anne about it and she said, "The alarm system is still on," and it still was. I said, "I'm going to go out and get the paper." I had to take the car down to the corner newsstand about two miles away to get the paper. I opened the door to the garage and, to my astonishment, the garage door was wide open. That can't be, not with the alarm system still running. I turned off the alarm system and got in the car, started to back out, still not fully understanding what was going on. Electrical flashes started hitting my hands and my face inside the car. It scared the hell out of me. I thought the whole thing was about to blow up. I jumped out of the car and ran back in the house and said, "Anne, there's something wrong here. The garage door was wide open and the alarm system wasn't tripped." She said, "We need to call the alarm man," who lived right down the road, only a short distance away.

I telephoned him, "Something weird is going on here; our alarm system was not tripped and the garage door was wide open." He said, "I'll come look at it right away." He drove over. He said, "Whitley, there is a powerful magnetic field on your garage door switches, much more powerful than anything this equipment can generate. It is so powerful that even though the door is wide open the switches cannot be tripped." He showed me his magnetometer and the needle shot all the way over to the right. We tried to download information from the alarm system, but it did not work, it was all scrambled. After he replaced the switches, it worked fine.

Later that afternoon I started to notice pain in the left ear and then felt a lump. After a few days the ear would turn bright red and I would hear a medium-pitched grinding noise. I did not know what was going on, but I did know about implants and I was terrified that they had put one of these damned things in me. What am I going to do about this? This is horrifying! Annie wanted me to leave it in. She said, "Let's figure out what it is and what it does and see if we can use it in some way." I was very paranoid about it as you may imagine. I left it in for about a year, two years maybe. It turned on and off and on and off.

We lost the cabin because we had run out of money and ended up in a little condo in San Antonio, Texas, which I had purchased during my mother's lifetime. We met Dr. William Mallow who was the head of Materials Science at Southwest Research in San Antonio and told him about the implant. Dr. Roger Leir was studying implants that were removed from other witnesses during this time. One afternoon at Dr. Mallow's office, my implant turned on. When it turns on the ear gets bright red and very hot; it's obviously emitting some kind of signal. There was a very sophisticated signal acquisitions lab at Southwest. We rushed into that lab; they picked up a signal and Bill told me it was the most unusual signal they had ever picked up. He wouldn't tell me anything more about it because most of the lab's equipment was classified.

Two years ago I was at the San Antonio Public Library Foundation as one of the honorees. Some men walked up to me and said they had been present when Dr. Mallow had recorded the signal. They just wanted me to know that it was still under study as one of the most unusual signals they had ever recorded, [and] then they walked away without another word. Now I use the implant every day of my life. It's turned into a tool, an appliance that I'm very familiar with. Annie was absolutely right: it should have stayed. At one point we did try to get it taken out.

Mishlove: In fact, as I recall, you wrote that at least a piece of it did get removed.

Strieber: Yes, that's right. When the doctor tried to remove it he touched it with the edge of a scalpel and it moved from inside my ear into the earlobe. He said, "I can't take it out without cutting off your whole ear." He pulled out a piece and closed up the little injury there. He had the little corner of it taken to a lab. The lab reported that it was a sliver of metal with motile, proteinaceous cilia coming out of it. In other words, it's a biomechanical piece of technology. A couple of days after the attempted surgery it came up from the earlobe back up to the top of my ear, where it stays today.

Mishlove: So, the original piece that was removed, that little corner to which you referred, has that been kept?

Strieber: It ended up at Southwest Research but apparently disappeared. Bill said, "I'll give it back to you." I went out to get it and he opened the drawer of his desk and he said, "Hm, it's gone. I've lost it." I don't know who has it, but obviously it wasn't lost. It disappeared into this enormous complicated, classified system that studies this stuff, unfortunately.

Mishlove: At this point, the story sounds very high tech. They got through your alarm system; they created a very mysterious magnetic field; they implanted a metallic device into your ear that was able to move around by itself.

Strieber: Through the skin, with no opening; there was no injury. There was just redness there. There was no cut.

Mishlove: So far it would seem as if we're dealing with some sort of high tech visitors. But as the story unfolds it's very clear that it has to do with the afterlife; it has to do with shamanistic like occurrences; that it's much more than simply technology.

Strieber: Colonel Philip Corso was criticized for publishing a book about his UFO knowledge right before he died. He was immediately, furiously debunked, primarily because he was probably telling the truth. The reason I think that is, first, I knew him and he was a very sincere guy. Second, he said something terribly important. He said that he had been in a situation in a cave where he'd had a brief face to face contact with one of these beings who wanted to leave the area in a machine of theirs. They couldn't leave because there was too much radar in use there and they wanted to have the radar turned off for ten minutes. Corso's response was, "In the military, ten minutes can be an eternity. What's in it for us? What do we get for doing that?" The answer was, "A new world if you can take it."

That, I think, is the defining statement; however it came into Philip Corso's head, it doesn't even matter, that's the truth: *a new world if you can take it.* It will not be given to us for [a] very good reason. But, if we can take it, if we can wrest the information out of their hands, and if we can bear what we find, what we're going to find is that the whole barrier between the living and the dead breaks down. Suddenly, you're living in an entirely different reality because the soul *does* exist. It isn't something to be sneered at and laughed at. It's actually the reason we are here and the reason we are of interest. It isn't because of our intelligence, which is a high moderate on the scale of intelligence in this universe. What is interesting about us is our ability to move our attention and our deep physicality, because our souls are here absorbing an enormous amount of physical experience and being altered by it very dramatically, and that's unusual. So, to them, we're an interesting specimen.

Mishlove: I'd like to come back to the implant, if we can. You say you're using it now, and have been for some years. How does it work? How do you use it?

Strieber: It's really very interesting. First of all, it doesn't give a damn if I'm going to the grocery store. It's not a tracking device. I'll give you a perfect example—this is recent. I'm always wanting to test it. I know the implant is there. I know the implant is real but am I actually using it or am I just deluding myself? So, I said to the implant," I want to know something. You teach me something that I know nothing whatsoever about but that is critically important to the new book I'm writing." It doesn't speak, instead it will open a slit in my eye where I can see typed writing racing past in the slit very quickly, but I can't read it except for an occasional snatch because it's moving too fast. I can't see it easily, unless I have a white background. But that's because this is subliminal information. It's not going into my conscious intellect; it's going somewhere deeper. So, the next day, I began to cogitate; something happened involving the number 137. I knew nothing about the significance of that number at that time.

Mishlove: It's a very significant number to me.

Strieber: To you it is, yes. But it wasn't to me. I didn't even know it existed. Finally, I googled this number. The whole mystery of the fine-structure constant exploded into my consciousness. I was led to Wolfgang Pauli and his relationship with Carl Jung and right to the mysterious line between the mystical and the scientific on which the fine-structure constant lies. In other words, probably the most crucial piece of information for the book I'm working on. That's how the implant works. Isn't that cool?

Mishlove: That's fascinating. I have been fascinated by that number for decades. Actually, I don't think I've done any interviews specifically on it, but one could. There's just an encyclopedia of information that comes out of that one number.

Strieber: We don't know why that number is that number and not another number, basically. It is the distance between the spectral lines in a spectrograph that are emitted by electrons. Is that correct?

Mishlove: I'm not a physicist myself. I believe it's related to the ratio of the weak force in physics to the electromagnetic force.

Strieber: That's a better way of putting it. In any case, we don't know why it is. But we do know that the universe would not work the same way it does if it was any other number.

Mishlove: That's right. At the same time, it's kind of an arbitrary number, but without it human life, or life of any kind wouldn't exist in our universe.

Strieber: It's not something like the Plank constant, which we can understand. It is the minimum possible distance between two separate objects without them linking. But the fine-structure constant is a mystery; it's arbitrary.

Mishlove: My friend Saul-Paul Sirag, who was a physicist and mathematician, based a lot of his own work on that number, so that would be a place I would point our viewers. I've done five interviews with him about his theoretical work. One could go into great depths into string theory, and hyperdimensional space. It has a great deal to do with the mathematical foundations of reality as we know it.

Strieber: Here is another story about the implant and its workings. I asked my discarnate wife, who I am in occasional pretty clear contact with, who would win the 2020 election, in September prior to the election in November. She said, "Trump," immediately. And I thought, "Oh god, this is my imagination. That's the worst possible outcome. It can't be true." Clinton was well ahead in the polls and Trump was not expected to win. Lo and behold, he did win.

At the time Trump won, I suddenly became aware that an enormous amount of intimate information about Adolf Hitler was coming into my mind from somewhere. I've read William Shirer's book and a few other books about World War II. In most histories of World War II, Hitler plays a huge role, but I've never read a biography of Hitler. But I became aware of very intimate details of Hitler's inner life. So, I thought to myself, "I could make a book out of this." It had to be a novel because I didn't have any particularly specific data.

I began to write it as a memoir of a man, who is now old, he's writing in the 1970s. He was a young wealthy German American, who became Hitler's confidant in 1931 before it was clear what Hitler actually was and what he was doing. As the war progressed and he realized how dangerous Hitler was as he became a spy for the Allies. At first he spied just for Churchill, then for the Allied cause. The book has got the most intimate portrait of Adolf Hitler ever written. I couldn't publish it under my name though. No one would buy it because it's by Whitley Strieber, that's a nasty no-no name in the publishing business now...

Mishlove: You've got forty books out. I'm surprised to hear that.

Strieber: There has been such a hardening against this whole UFO thing in the past five or six years, it's unbelievable. They won't touch UFOs even though the subject is extremely popular. My name is associated with that, not with historical novels also, so that was another problem. So, I published it myself under an open pseudonym of Jonathan White Lane and it's called, *In Hitler's House: The Memoir of William Weber*. It was an extraordinary experience to have written it. I even found out what toothpaste Hitler used. It was extraordinary. I could think of nothing that I needed that didn't come to me through the implant which is very indirect. I can't expect a direct answer but if I wait, well, what I need comes.

Mishlove: Were you able to validate any of this information? Like the toothpaste?

Strieber: I validated it all. That's the thing. This information would float into my head then I'd do research about it. I validated the information from a little book that had been written in German by Hitler's personal valet. I got a copy of it and I had a German speaker translate it for me. Indeed, it was exactly as I had already discovered.

Mishlove: To shift a little bit, you mentioned that you're in communication with your late wife Anne.

Strieber: At times, yes.

Mishlove: Is that also in any way related to the implant?

Strieber: I think it probably is and I'll tell you why. While I was writing the Hitler book, my writing got much better. It had really taken a new step forward. The implant was working overtime. There in the little slit, the words were sailing past at breakneck speed. I finally asked it, "Who are you?" because it seemed different; it was much better than it had ever been before. Very slowly and clearly it came across in the slit, "It's me, Anne."

Mishlove: She is the one of course who encouraged you to keep the implant.

Strieber: Anne was my muse while she was alive, and so incredibly important to everything. She's the one who named the book *Communion*. She said, "That's what it's about." When I finally got up the guts to tell Anne what I thought had happened to me, she didn't react the way you would think. Anne didn't say, "Oh my god, Whitley. I'm concerned about our son because this is a deep end of the pool thing, this is very serious. I want you to see a psychiatrist and I don't want to hear anything more about this." She said, "Oh really? Well, that's interesting. We can do a lot with this." That was how *Communion* started. Anne's presence was important in the writing of that book, every word of it, she edited it in detail. It was as if Anne was there to do this. She was absolutely made for it.

Mishlove: One of the things that you report is that after *Communion* came out—it was a huge international bestseller at the time—you received hundreds of thousands of letters from people who had had similar experiences.

Strieber: That's correct. Anne took that in hand because she could read very quickly. She would read a complex novel in an afternoon quite easily. She read them, cataloged them, and kept the ones with complex stories and let the others that just said, "Well, thank you for the book," go out. She ended up with about 9 or 10 boxes of letters, which are now at Rice University in the collection that Jeff Kripal is supervising. Even if the visitors don't exist, those letters represent one of the best collections of folkloric narrative in the world. Anne did all of that. I always like to speak of her contribution because it's a very important one. Maybe the most important part of it happened one day when she walked out of her office with a bemused look on her face and said, "Whitley, this has something to do with what we call death." It changed everything, *everything*, at that moment because I realized that contact with the visitors and contact with the dead is the same thing, essentially.

Mishlove: At least it would seem as if they're related. They could be different phenomena that have some sort of connection with each other.

Strieber: That's what I mean, actually. The visitors don't have a barrier between the living and the dead, unless they are us in another form. That is also a real possibility because nature is prolific in creating multi-formed species. Maybe we are one. How could the caterpillar ever imagine the butterfly? Ever? Or the tadpole, the frog? And yet, there it is.

Mishlove: It's certainly easy to imagine. Olaf Stapledon, the great science fiction writer, talks about in his novels the many different transmutations that the human species might go through.

Strieber: I believe he does. I haven't read Stapledon in so long. In any case, this is not a decided thing. It's a wonderful, fabulous question because on the one hand we're talking about the nonphysical side of it, on the other hand I'm close to people who study some extremely strange materials, like Jacques Vallée. These materials can't exist in this universe, and yet here they are. They supposedly came from a UFO crash site.

Mishlove: You're talking about physical materials.

Strieber: I am talking about the possibility that this may be about communication with the dead and the implant is to a degree that, but it's a physical thing. That's the wonder and delight of this question. That's what makes it so much fun to be in the place I'm in in the world because I like questions. My wife said, after she died, "The human species is too young to have beliefs. We need to stick with the questions." I love that statement because if you look at our history, it is a history of battling and fighting and killing each other over beliefs. Whose belief is right? My belief is right and I believe that and I'm going to kill you because you don't believe it. It's happening right now in Syria, it's what ISIS is all about, it's what Wahhabism is all about, it's what the Church was all about throughout the Middle Ages.

Mishlove: People also commit suicide because of their beliefs. Beliefs are very powerful, there's no question about it. What you're suggesting is if we're going to understand this phenomenon we would do well to let go of all our preconceptions.

Strieber: Letting go of belief is the most freeing thing in the world. You say, "I know I don't know." The mind wants to fill that gap. It wants to say, "No, no, no, you can't look at this and say you don't know what it is. That looks like a flying saucer; that must be from another planet. It's from Zeta Reticuli; it's the Greys; it's the Reptilians; you better watch out for them." Soon, you have this whole cosmology and folklore all mixed up in your head and you begin to live it as if it were real. But we don't know.

Mishlove: You're known as a writer of horror novels. Some of the experiences that you've had also are reminiscent of horror novels. I'm thinking of the experience of the giant spiders in the bedroom above your wife.

Strieber: I couldn't put that in a horror novel; it was too scary.

Mishlove: It's funny to me because you seem to love your life; you enjoy these experiences, but honestly some of them are horrific.

Strieber: The reason the visitors have become so connected with me is that I am amused and entertained by horror. Fear is fascinating to me and I am perfectly capable of experiencing fear without rejecting it, which I do all the time. Recently,

I did it a couple of times in pretty intense situations. But, with regard to the spiders, that was a very, very interesting experience. At the time, I was having intimate contact with a group who would come to the cabin very noisily and drop down onto the roof of my meditation room that I had there. They would then come in through the roof. I could feel their presence but they were not visible. I couldn't meditate with them unless I could see them, so one of them made himself visible briefly. Annie once came into the room to meditate with them too, but when the crash, crash, crash and all the thudding on the roof came, she said, "Actually, I'm not ready for this," and she left.

One night they began paging through my mind, and I would see images of my life one page after another. I guess it was like one of those life reviews they talk about when you're dying. They stopped at a moment in which I had been attracted to a woman other than Anne. Being a man, if a beautiful woman comes up to me and flirts with me I'm going to react like all heterosexual men do. But that doesn't necessarily mean I'm going to abandon my wife or cheat on her. That wasn't good enough for them. They saw this and didn't like it.

Later that night I woke up and the entire roof of the cabin was gone. There was something behind it, a blackness, not the universe of stars as we know it; it's another blackness that you don't want to look at for long, which was very hard. I could see these people peering at me from around the edges and I thought, "This can't be good." Then they made me fall asleep again immediately.

I woke up sometime later and, to my absolute horror, there were these gigantic spiders clinging to the now reappeared cathedral ceiling. They were about a good foot, foot and a half long, with huge black shiny abdomens with tiger stripes on them. They were very, very disappointing things to find hanging above your bed in the middle of the night. I thought, "Oh god, this must be some sort of a nightmare. But I could hear them and I could also see that one of them was scratching across the wood as if it was going to fall off on Anne who was sleeping beside me peacefully. I thought, "God, what am I going to do?" I wanted to get out of the bed and run out of there, desperately. I got up, turned and looked. Now I was standing up wide-awake. The spiders are still there and the one hanging over Anne is in more trouble than it was before. I forced myself to go around that bed to lie on top of her so that [it] would not fall on my girl. They disappeared. It was a test. Are you really in love? You discover right now, tonight, how you feel; what is your real link to this woman? Now they knew, my real link to this woman is that I would give my life for her. I really would.

Mishlove: That's a very powerful experience, obviously, even remembering it now you're still a bit shaken by it. I can see that.

Strieber: Oh yeah.

Mishlove: Any psychologist would say that what seems to have occurred here is an externalization of your own inner emotions around the memory of a woman who had once tempted you and some lingering guilt around that. Your own inner psyche managed to externalize itself into the room where you were, in the form of those spiders.

Strieber: Yes, unless it was drawn out of me or given to me from someone else. I don't know, but that's certainly a very valid possibility. There are lots of possibilities, though. I perceive it as something that was done to me so I could discover my real bond to my wife, which is still to this day extremely strong. I'm still married. I wear both rings because, in my estimation, we're still together but we just have one body left and I happen to be the one running it.

Mishlove: That's a beautiful way of putting it. It also brings to light the emotional component around these experiences. So many parapsychologists like myself like to think in terms of experimental design, proofs, and we neglect the emotions. But because of your background in literature, you have a deep appreciation for that and I think the scientific community would do very well to pay attention to these things.

Strieber: It's an interesting question about the scientific community. Science proceeds on the study of what it can measure. In the present situation there's something here that's very big. I think it's probably much bigger than us. I think that we are part of it. It is not part of us, but we cannot measure it. Maybe that's because it does not wish to be measured. Maybe because it's highly conscious, highly intelligent and does not want us to gain a foothold in our relationship with it. It wants us to remain as we are, more or less, supplicants, and unable to really realize it in our own minds, in terms of science I mean, because science can't measure it. In terms of the individual emotional experience, and the academic exploration of the culture that we can work with, that we have.

Mishlove: It's a very elusive phenomenon but I was also fascinated by several of the reports that you wrote about when, after the publication of *Communion,* different groups of people would come to visit you and stay overnight in your cabin in the hope of actually having some experiences themselves, and often they did.

Strieber: Oh, they did. Annie was the one who selected the people. She knew who would have experiences and who wouldn't from reading their letters. I don't know how she knew but every once in a while she would put a letter aside. I asked her once, "What are these letters you put aside?" She said, "Those are people who are coming to the cabin." In fact, the first group had about six or seven people. Among them was the editor of a big magazine then called *New Age Magazine.* He had promised that he would write about the experience and make it a cover story in the magazine. The group encountered the little dark blue figures that at times seem rather comical but are actually not all that funny when you get to know them.

Mishlove: You call them the kobolds.

Strieber: Kobolds are what they were called in Bavaria. Large parts of Bavaria have many tunnels, too small for a human being to have carved out. People used to see these dark, small figures in mines in that part of the world. That's why I call them kobolds because they wore cobalt blue work suits. In any case, there were four people, including this editor, sleeping in the living room on cots and on a convertible couch. The Kobolds immobilized them but they could still talk to each other. Then these figures jumped around in the room so they could be seen.

Meanwhile, downstairs, the couple awoke and found, standing at the foot of the bed, a woman that they knew who had died in 1983 in the Mexico City earthquake. So, you had the supposed aliens in the living room and a dead person downstairs telling them that she was all right. So, what did it mean? That was the first group experience at the cabin. The editor wouldn't write about it because he was afraid it would ruin his career. It was unfortunate he didn't do that. It was a basic mistake. He had guaranteed to them he would write it and they came and he didn't. So, he's got that still in his life.

The second time the visitors showed up, we had Raven Dana, Laurie Barnes and another lady staying in the cabin. We also had a low light camera set up. Drew Cummings was staying in the living room on the convertible couch with his wife. He was a documentary filmmaker from LA. Raven was in one bedroom, and Laurie and the other lady were in another bedroom. Dora Ruffner, Ed Conroy and our son Andrew and I were all down in the woods sleeping. I stayed with my son because there was no other bed in the house; it was too full.

What happened that night was totally remarkable. Raven Dana woke up to find this being with big, black eyes coming in through the screen window, which was screwed closed. It touched her on the arm and then asked her, "What can I do for you?" She said, "You could go down that hall," which was where the camera was trained. The next thing we knew, the lady in the other bedroom and Laurie Barnes were both awakened by this being in the same way. It remained in that room briefly and then disappeared. Then, Drew Cummings woke up and saw a little man with a great big head leaning over the convertible couch. He had assumed this was all nonsense, that it wasn't real and suddenly here it was, quite real. He was horrified, whereupon it changed into a hawk and disappeared.

About an hour later, dawn came and Andrew and I decided to come back to the house. As we were walking up, we had a view of the house before us: the swimming pool, the deck and then a view across the yard that led into the woods. Out of the front door came a translucent, hooded figure about 3 feet tall, that walked down the deck, across the yard, and then shot across the woods dodging the trees at breakneck speed as we both stood there watching. We rushed into the house to see Drew Cummings and his wife on their feet because they had experienced, just moments before, a tremendous burst of heat as this being was leaving.

I talked about this event with a couple of scientists and they concluded that the reason the being became invisible was that it bent light around it so that it couldn't be seen, but in so doing created heat. There was technology in use as well as mystery there that night. Those are the two cabin stories. There were a couple of others but those were the two biggest ones with multiple witnesses.

Mishlove: Whatever became of the potential documentary film?

Strieber: We looked and looked at that recording from the low light camera. There wasn't a sign of anything, which was so frustrating. I have a surveillance camera in this house. I can always tell when something is going to happen during my meditations, even if I'm not going to perceive it, because the camera turns off. If it doesn't turn off, I don't get visitors.

Mishlove: How interesting. So, the camera is configured to do that.

Strieber: No, it's not configured to turn itself off; it just does it. In the morning when I looked at the footage, it said the camera was not turned on. It can be turned off in the software.

Mishlove: Speaking of your meditation practice, I learned in reading the book that even prior to the experience you wrote about in *Communion*, you were involved for I believe fifteen years with the Gurdjieff group.

Strieber: I was in the Gurdjieff Foundation for fifteen years. I still do the Gurdjieff work and some members of the foundation still consider me to be a member. I started in 1970 and I was taught something called the sensing exercise by Joseph Stein and William Segal who were teachers in the foundation. This exercise is a matter of moving your attention into your physical sensation, into your body, in a methodical way. I don't think the visitors would have showed up in my life if I hadn't done it. (A) I don't think they would have seen me, and (B) there would have been no basis for communication.

Back in September of 2015, just after Annie passed away, I was at a conference in Nashville with our friends William Henry, who does conferences on spiritual matters from time to time, and his wife Claire. At a break in the conference, a woman came up to me and said, "Mr. Strieber, the strangest thing just happened to me. I just want to tell you something and I don't quite know how to say this." I said, "Just go ahead and say it because I'm not going to be surprised by the strangeness of it, obviously, whatever it is." So she said, "Your wife Anne just talked to me. I heard her very clearly in my ear say, 'tell Whitley I can see him when he's in the chair.'" That meant a lot because she was referring to my sitting in the evenings doing the sensing exercise. I realized then why, years before, one of the visitors had said to me that they came because they saw a glow. I thought at the time they meant the glow of cities and so forth, but they didn't. They meant my glow.

When you place your attention on your nervous system, it increases the energy output and they can see that. When they see that, they know that this is a person who possesses a certain tool that they can use to communicate. They will sometimes come and become involved with me then. When I realized that with Annie, I started redoubling my efforts at meditation because I knew she was there. No sooner had I done that, than one night at 3:00 am, I was awakened by one of my toes being shocked. I leaped up but couldn't explain it. I went back to bed but then the next night something invisible grabbed my right nipple and shook it like the dickens. I barreled out of the bed that time because I thought someone was in the apartment but nobody was there. I thought to myself," Wait a minute, they've tried before to get me to meditate at 3:00 am; that's what this is about."

I performed the sensing exercise at 3:00 am and since then it has become a ritual. The last time they woke me up to do it was the night before last. They wake me up now by blowing in my face. Normally, I will wake up myself. I purposely don't use an alarm or anything like that. I want this to be more organic, because that's I how feel it should be. Last night I woke up myself at 3:00 am and meditated for about half an hour. It's very comfortable and I've been doing it since September of 2015 and I feel great.

Mishlove: I think it's a wonderful practice, meditating at 3 am. But I'm under the impression that it's not just meditation that's happening for you. Are you experiencing contacts during those meditations?

Strieber: I am quite often experiencing them. It is an intimate friendship now. There have been some contretemps, though. Back in February of 2018, I was begging and pleading with them to come out because I see our planet is dying and we don't know it. They have already told me about a climax of climate change, "It will come upon them unaware." It's made me crazy because I've got three beautiful grandkids. I want this place to last. I'm begging them and begging them to just come out publicly with me for fifteen minutes so we could change the world. They've also given me all kinds of information about how to fix the climate; that it takes a lot of work but we can do it, if we had the motive. Their presence in this would give us the motive.

They are very aware that we have a lot of trouble perceiving them when we are face to face with them. I admit that it's hard, even for me after thirty years of interaction. I wake up one night at 3:00 am and I'm aware that there's something in the bed between my legs. Now, I don't have cats or dogs; it's not going to be an animal from the outside. I thought, "Oh my god, it's one of them." It's within inches of my gonads in the most intimate spot in the bed that it could be in. Instinct took over. I leapt out of the bed. It leapt out with me and left a big gash on one of my calves, which I took pictures of. The visitor shot off out of the house. There I was with my answer: "If you can't take us, how can the others?" It was agonizing.

Later, I had been really thinking about Annie. I had been meditating very deeply and it felt as if she was with me. It was very powerful stuff for a few nights. Then, one night, I was just lying in bed after the eleven o'clock meditation, just about to go to sleep, when I felt a very gentle presence sit down on me, right over my genitals. Whatever is going on here is not modest. I thought to myself, "My god, one of them is sitting on me." I started to open my eyes, but then I thought, "No, don't do that yet." Because every time I try to look at them something goes wrong, like what had happened previously. So, I laid there and just let it happen. This incredible, sweet, beautiful energy filled my body. It was a lovely, lovely experience, so poignant and rich and delicious in a physical sense, it felt wonderful. And then gradually it faded and I opened my eyes to see a little dark figure dart off toward the ceiling.

After a while I went to sleep. I did the 3:00 am meditation, which was very deep and powerful. After that I proceeded to have what were not dreams. I was in other places. Of course, they weren't temples or heaven or anything. One of them appeared to be a kitchen. I always end up like that. I'm the guy, when I have an out-of-body experience, I'm living at the ordinary level of life. But this was not an out-of-body experience, nor was it a lucid dream. I was actually there for a couple of minutes.

Then I asked the implant, "What went on that night?" After a while I had the impression that I should telephone a certain woman that I know who's been to India. I described the intimate experience and she said, "Whitley, I can explain that completely. That was kundalini. I've had the same experience but it was induced in me in India by a certain guru and he accidentally healed one of my pierced ears." Then she said, "Whitley, it's something that is often followed by bilocation experiences. Did you have one?" I realized that I did. I bilocated into somebody's kitchen.

Mishlove: This is such a rich story; we could pursue it in many different dimensions. I would like to come back to the female figure that you reported on in *Communion*. You reported that you actually did have one or two sexual experiences.

Strieber: I sure did.

Mishlove: Your wife Anne didn't show any jealousy about this.

Strieber: No, not at all. Anne just rolled with it. She was perfectly happy for me to have these experiences, and they were incredible. One of them took place in the guest room in our house in upstate New York. I woke up and I was lying on my back with the most fantastic erection you could imagine and I was already inside the body of this being, this woman, who was sitting on me, and proceeded to have a fiery, unbelievably intense sexual experience. The room was full of people, one of whom I recognized. They seemed very embarrassed to be there. I couldn't see the woman's face—it was blacked out—but I could see the rest of her body. It was just a very, very, very powerful experience. It was so delightful that it almost would have burned me out if it kept on for very long.

But here's a fascinating story about the man I saw standing there. Just about four years ago, I met a gentleman from Romania who had only one unusual experience in his life. During the experience he had a mystery story written in Romanian with him. He didn't remember the experience at all but he was asked to underline a certain name in this book. He didn't know why. He could only remember that. I said, "Well, what was the name?" It was the name of the man who was in the room that night. The Romanian said to me that this man had seen something and had been told that he must never tell anyone what he saw.

I've talked to the man since then and I've said, you know, I seem to remember you up at my cabin. He says, "No, I don't think I was ever there." I said, "Yeah, I believe you were; don't you remember coming up there?" "No," he said, "I don't." If you get a chance to live like this, you can either take it one of two ways. You can fall in love with it or you can curl up into a fetal position and pray to God it goes away. I fell in love with it. I fell in love with her. There are two pictures on my wall: my wife and her [shows framed image of *Communion* cover]. They are my constant companions when I'm working; the two of them.

Mishlove: That is the picture that you had painted for the cover of *Communion*.

Strieber: That is the original picture.

Mishlove: When I read through *The Supernatural* I noticed that you referred to that picture twice. Once you wrote that you had painted it and another time you wrote that you had *had* it painted.

Strieber: Oh no, I didn't paint it. I had it painted. I sat beside the artist while he painted it.

Mishlove: Maybe it's a typo, but it implied that you were really involved.

Strieber: Heavily involved. Every single brush stroke came from me. That is a portrait from my memory.

Mishlove: Jeff Kripal, when I interviewed him about another book he wrote, *Secret Body*...

Strieber: Which is an incredible book.

Mishlove: He refers of course to *The Supernatural*, in that book. He says that to him, as a scholar of religion, that is an image of a Hindu goddess. I think he was referring to Kali.

Strieber: I wouldn't be surprised if she was Kali because she does a lot of very Kali-like things. She had a relationship with my wife, a very friendly and comfortable relationship. I had the sense that they might be both the same being, that Anne and this being might be combined.

Mishlove: That would make sense.

Strieber: Anne was very connected to her. Some of the sexual experiences were really intimate and lovely. They were wonderful if you don't mind a rather dominating female presence, which I got used to quite quickly. She called all the shots. I was just there.

Mishlove: I think it's unusual that for some reason she didn't want you to see her face at those moments.

Strieber: I think that might have turned me off. She's a lot prettier in the portrait than she is in real life. Bruce Lee, who was an editor at William Morrow, saw her face to face in a bookstore in Manhattan. He never stopped talking about her eyes. The black eyes that are in the painting, they could be removed like dark glasses and there would be someone else under there. I don't know what they are. But, she has blue eyes that take you into another world. Bruce Lee said he had never experienced anything as powerful as the loathing in her eyes. I don't experience that. When I've seen her naked, I have seen something so desirable that it's agonizing—agonizing. I can't take it for long because I want to merge with it. It's overwhelming. I couldn't have made love to her for two more minutes if I had been engaged with those eyes. That's why the blackness was there.

Mishlove: You also mention that it was Anne who came up with the title for that book, *Communion*, really implying that this is a very spiritual relationship.

Strieber: I was going to call it *Body Terror* because it was the most terrifying thing that had ever happened to me. Suddenly, in the middle of the night one night, Anne was three quarters asleep and she says, "*Communion*, you should call it *Communion* because that's what it's about." I wasn't absolutely sure who was talking. I said to myself, "Yeah, I will call it *Communion* then."

Mishlove: Because for you the initial experience was practically like—and you used that word—being raped?

Strieber: I was raped. I had an object inserted into my rectum and I jerked around and struggled so much that I tore my rectum. The scar is still there. I still feel it. The pain isn't too bad right now, but it can vary; it can get very bad. I've got medicine for it, to reduce the pain, that I use frequently.

Mishlove: You're suffering from that injury after 30 years.

Strieber: Yeah, it's a big scar, it's significant. My rectum was torn.

Mishlove: You have an amazing ability to take a frightening, painful, horrific experience and to see it in the most positive light.

Strieber: Annie used to say, "I signed on for an interesting life and I've got my wish." I feel exactly the same way. I'm fascinated with them. I think they might be quite dangerous but I'm also crazy about them. I meditate with them all the time now and I'm very happy with this. Recently, they wanted me to write a certain book. I had a script I wanted to write and a different book. When I started to write the other book, there was a type of complex communication that made it very clear that that other book was a mistake for me to write. I thought about working on the script and the same kind of communication came again.

I thought, "Maybe I better work on the book." Once I started working on the book, the beautiful kundalini experience that I described earlier occurred.

So, it's very much a reward-based and threat-based kind of scenario. They're very overstated, I think, but that's fine by me. If that's the way they are, that's the way they are. Maybe that's the way I am because ultimately the barriers that we imagine between ourselves and them are more or less illusory.

Mishlove: In fact, you've suggested many times that they are us, perhaps from the future.

Strieber: My problem with that is time is not a force. We have four forces in this universe that we know of. Entropy is what gives us the illusion of duration. We know gravity as a force but time isn't a force. There is something there that we don't understand. Einstein's observations, when he was a young man trying to get the clocks synchronized on the Swiss railway system, would not be true because, in fact, they do run at different speeds in different places. Time is not fixed like the speed of light. The speed of time is malleable. But I still wonder. It's easy to say they're from the future. The truth is that we are much larger than we think and that these bodies are projections. This is why the first thing that Annie said when we re-contacted each other, "It's a game, Whitley."

Mishlove: Speaking of the game, earlier you spoke with great passion about wanting to personally be instrumental in helping to address the problem of climate change and many other disasters that are being built up on this planet right now because of human activity. Do you still intend to do that?

Strieber: I can't, though I've wanted to for years. They started to come into my life in the early 1980s, I think, resulting in the writing of *War Day* and *Nature's End*. *Nature's End* was scoffed at by the environmental community at the time. But if you read it now, it reads like something that is actually happening. In fact, it is happening. Then there came *The Key*, which laid out the whole mechanism of sudden climate change that led to the writing of *The Coming Global Superstorm*. But *Superstorm* was denigrated again by the environmental community because they wanted to see it as something more gradual. The suddenness is too disturbing, I guess.

If you look at the geologic record, you find that there are instances when these changes occur very suddenly. It's like a rubber band that stretches and stretches and suddenly snaps. The problem with that is, it suddenly snaps and then it's a new climate regime that lasts for hundreds of thousands or millions of years. When that happens this time, I don't think that the planet is going to have a system capable of supporting this huge human population. We are at the top of a bell curve and we are going to go down the other side very rapidly. I know it's ridiculous, but I learned from the visitors that you don't think of people, you think of individuals. You have to keep in your mind at all times that everybody feels of themself the same way that you do of yourself. That each of us is all we have.

That makes me desperate to make some kind of a dent in this madness. We have a president (Trump) saying he doesn't believe the science of climate change and a large population who, out of their inner terror, follow him. He's got a soul that's in deep jeopardy. That always troubles me, because I have seen what happens. This is about the soul, this journey, and it's a test and you can fail it. I don't want anyone to fail it. I don't want Donald Trump to fail this test. I don't want any human being to fail this test. I want us to have joy, all of us. I don't think of it in terms of, "Oh, that person is evil so I hate him." I think in terms of, "That person is making a mistake and I've got to help him somehow."

Mishlove: Whitley Strieber, I really appreciate your heartfelt sentiments. I happen to share them. I have to say, I think Jeffrey Kripal was wrong when he said that you're not like a Biblical prophet. I think in many ways you are.

Strieber: Here I am, biblical prophet. I can cook a pretty good bouillabaisse; I'll tell you that.

Mishlove: Whitley, this has truly been a joy and an eye opener for me.

Strieber: Thank you.

Mishlove: I'm very grateful to have had this time with you and I'm hopeful we can continue the conversation because I suspect we've just scratched the surface and I think the more that we can contribute to the global conversation that's happening and keep these ideas on people's minds, the better it will be for the planet.

Strieber: I'd like to be able to come to Albuquerque and do it face to face.

Mishlove: I would love to have you here for a stay where we can really go into more depth.

Strieber: Well, thank you very much.

Mishlove: Thank you for being with me, Whitley.

8

A New Vision of the Unexplained: Part 2
with
Jeffrey Kripal

~

Jeffrey Mishlove: This is part two of, "A New Vision of the Unexplained." My guest today is Professor Jeffrey Kripal who is the J. Newton Rayzor Professor of Philosophy and Religious Thought and the former chair of the Department of Religious Studies at Rice University in Houston, Texas. He is co-author with Whitley Strieber of *The Supernatural: A New Vision of the Unexplained.* He is also co-author with Elizabeth Krohn of *Changed in a Flash: One Woman's Near-Death Experience and Why a Scholar Thinks It Empowers Us All.* In addition, he has written *Authors of the Impossible: The Paranormal and the Sacred*; *Mutants and Mystics: Science Fiction, Superhero Comics and the Paranormal*; *Kali's Child: The Mystical and Erotic in the Life and Teachings of Ramakrishna*; and *Secret Body: Erotic and Esoteric Currents in the History of Religions.*

Once again we'll be reviewing this incredible adventure that Whitley Strieber has been on now for over three decades. I should think for a person such as yourself, a historian of religion, this is the equivalent of being with a real, live religious phenomenon.

Jeffrey Kripal: That's certainly how it feels. It's one of the reasons why I'm so committed to it. It's quite the thing to watch, and frankly, to interact with. It's like being in the front row of a really good Super Bowl. Yet unlike being at the Super Bowl because all you can do is holler and yell and nothing really changes on the field. When Whitley and I talk, things change and he responds. It's kind of a living, morphing thing that's happening.

Mishlove: I haven't counted, but there does seem to be a really wide variety of different phenomena that occur in his presence: materializations, out-of-body experiences, sexual experiences, lights, and sounds.

Kripal: Yeah, he's radioactive.

Mishlove: And a wide variety of entities or creatures seem to appear.

Kripal: It's extraordinary. John Keel would call it a Disneyland of the paranormal, though that's putting it too dismissively. Usually, with other people, I don't witness paranormal events; I hear about them secondhand. But with him, I experienced it as well.

Mishlove: You've experienced things in his presence yourself?

Kripal: Yes, I have. It's complicated to talk about because some of it's so personal and involves other people. I regularly invite Whitley to Esalen to these symposia I lead and occasionally we'll share a room. He always jokes, "Well, you may not want to do that," and we laugh about it but, joking aside, things have happened. Usually, when these things happen to Whitley, he's the sole witness. Other people may see strange things, but they don't see what Whitley sees.

He's often awakened in the middle of the night by these visitors, as he calls them, and then he sits in a chair and meditates, usually around three or four in the morning. This is very apparent if you're his roommate and, on some level, I knew that this was happening every night.

One night when I was asleep, it felt like I had split off into a second personality and I heard myself say, "Oh, my God." This other part of me was witnessing whatever was going on, over by Whitley, and it was shocked and terrified, but my sleeping self was completely clueless, which was very weird. That split was not subtle. There was a part of me that was clearly witnessing something and the other part of me was hearing what it said but had zero access to it otherwise. I was two distinct subjects at that moment, and I'd never experienced anything like that.

A little later that same night, I heard, in my head, something crash and fall but I wasn't sure that it was in the room. The crash was so loud it woke me up so I looked all around the room and saw that nothing had fallen; nothing had broken. Within about two hours, some part of me had witnessed something that the other part of me hadn't and something had mimicked or replicated a crash. The next morning I, told Whitley about it. He explained that he had experienced the visitors again. I don't know if that was a direct experience that I had but it was definitely not an experience that this Jeff that you're talking to right now had.

Mishlove: It's very personal, but I don't think it would count very much in a parapsychological discussion of evidence.

Kripal: No, it's not evidence at all but it was my experience, and I don't need the evidence. Something happened around a sleeping Whitley Strieber that was inexplicable.

Mishlove: As I read through the book, one of the most fascinating aspects of it was your discussion of the distinction between imaginary and imaginal and how that pertains to Whitley's experiences.

Kripal: The thing that prevents us as a culture from really understanding the experiences of these sorts of individuals

New Thinking Allowed Dialogues

is that we lack any real theory of the imagination. All that we believe in our culture is that that which is imagined is imaginary and then gets dismissed as purely subjective hallucination or illusion. The more you look at these things, the more you begin to suspect that sometimes the imagination is the organ of mediation of whatever is in the environment that is communicating to you or to the subject. What's being imagined is not apparent but something is really there in this weird, real-unreal, zone. To me, if we can move in that direction, I think we'll be much smarter about these things. We won't interpret them literally, necessarily, but we also won't dismiss them.

Mishlove: You refer to the biological origin of the word *imaginal*, that it had something to do, when it was conceived of by various philosophers like Henry Corbin, as a way in which the caterpillar becomes a butterfly.

Kripal: Right. People who know about the category of the imaginal think that it was coined by Henry Corbin, who was this really gifted French historian of Persian mysticism and Sufism who achieved prominence in the mid 20th century He was a student of Louis Massignon, another really fascinating and great historian of Sufism. Corbin used this category of the imaginal throughout his work to describe this mediating space—what he called the intermediate world. For him, it was very real, but it was also visionary. He lived and thought in this intermediary world.

In fact, he didn't coin the term or invent it at all. It had already been used fairly extensively by previous writers, including—help me out here Jeffrey ...

Mishlove: Frederic Myers.

Kripal: Frederic Myers is the original, but there was also a French psychiatrist who wrote a book called *From India to the Planet Mars*.

Mishlove: Theodore Flournoy.

146

Kripal: Flournoy had used it well before Corbin had and he had tutored Jung. Jung got it from Flournoy, but Flournoy got it from Frederic Myers who, I think, is the original source of this term. He was a Victorian British classicist and psychical researcher who thought that these organs of cognition are evolving very gradually in the species. He got this idea from nineteenth century entomologists who distinguished between the larval stage of an insect and the imaginal stage of an insect. The larval stage was the gooey caterpillar crawling around on the leaf and eating the plant. The imago, the perfect image, or the imaginal form of the insect was, in this case, the butterfly.

When Myers described telepathy, apparitions of the dead, and precognition as *imaginal* forms of experience, he meant this in the evolutionary sense of the word as something moving from a larval, immature stage to a more perfect, developed stage.

Mishlove: If we apply that to human beings such as ourselves— you, me, and Whitley—the suggestion is that there's further evolution ahead for the human species, and that these experiences may be part of an evolutionary process.

Kripal: Myers believed that what he called supernormal experiences—which we now call paranormal, but it's very much related—were plant buds that were trying to appear through the dirt. Myers told this funny story of all of these caterpillars sitting around chewing on their leaf, and this beautiful butterfly lands, and the caterpillars are like, "What the hell? What's that?" They have no conception that they will eventually mature into this flying winged thing that looks nothing like them. That's what Myers really felt about this whole realm we're talking about.

That's what Whitley suggests a lot in his own writings. He sees the visitors as essentially the butterfly landing on the leaf with the caterpillars, and we're like, "What the hell? What is this?" But it's actually us; we just don't recognize it as us.

Mishlove: Whitley is also quite convinced that these experiences he's been having are really physical.

Kripal: That's where I hesitate, not because I don't believe Whitley, but because it breaks all of our models. I think our inclination is to consider it as subjective, mental, or spiritual, but what Whitley is saying is, "No, this *physically* happened to me. Someone was *physically* in my room; they did *physical* things to me; they *physically* put an implant in my ear right here," and then he points to it and shows you when it turns red. These are *physical* things for him, not just spiritual.

Mishlove: I was particularly impressed by one story in which— it's very complex—but at the end of the story, he sees some large spiders, a foot wide or a foot and a half wide on the ceiling of his room. He feels that he has to protect his wife, who's in bed next to him, from these spiders, and he jumps on top of her, which for him is a demonstration that he's willing to risk his life for his wife. That's how he feels emotionally about it. But then once he's done that and satisfied the need to demonstrate that to himself, they disappear.

Kripal: Would Anne have seen those spiders if she woke up? Probably not.

Mishlove: But it does seem to me that Whitley is quite sincere when he says, for him, they're very tangible.

Kripal: There's no question. The man is not lying. He's not making stuff up. He's trying to be honest with his readers about what he experienced, what he saw, what he felt, what was done to him. The question of honesty is answered in my mind, just because I know Whitley.

Mishlove: I think we ought to address it a little bit because he's such a talented writer and he had a history of writing horror novels. I think he's very gifted at just telling the story and embellishing it in such a captivating way that the temptation is to think that maybe his creative faculties have gotten the best of him, and that this is just another wonderful mystery that he's creating.

Kripal: I think there are two things to say. I really believe these experiences *are* about his literary genius. I think they're intimately linked to his creativity and the production of the novels and the books. I'm in the process of reading hundreds and eventually thousands of personal accounts of abduction experiences by people all across the United States, Europe, Canada, and Mexico, from all walks of life. What strikes me about so many of these accounts is how badly they're written because most people can't write, Jeffrey. That's just an observation; it's not a judgment. A lot of these accounts don't even make grammatical sense. So, when you read them, it's hard to take the experiences seriously because the form they're in is such a mess.

I also know on another level that the literary form or dis-form of the expression may have nothing to do with the genuineness and power of the original experience. I think we confuse those. When you get someone like Whitley Strieber, who, not only has hundreds of these extraordinary experiences, but is also a professional writer, you get this wow effect which seems suspicious. I think we should have the opposite response that we finally have someone who can articulate their experiences because that's really rare. I think we should consider Whitley's books as literary gifts that are precise and accurate in a way that other accounts aren't.

Mishlove: You list several reasons why you accept Whitley's experiences as authentic. One of them is that when he had his initial contact back in 1985, there was a huge UFO flap going on in upstate New York for decades prior to that. His experiences fit into a well-known context.

Kripal: I don't have any doubt that these things happened to Whitley, not just because of that Hudson Valley century-long context, but also millennia of religious experiences of strange creatures coming from the sky and doing even stranger things to us. This is nothing new. This is as old as it gets. This is as universal as it gets. This is as religious as it gets. None of that means I believe the mythologies or the religions that spin out of these experiences. I don't, actually. What I was trying to articulate in the book was this paradoxical position that I think we need to inhabit, where we recognize that these are real experiences, but we want to be smarter about how they are turned into cultures, religions, and civilizations.

Mishlove: In an earlier conversation, you and I talked about your recent book, *Secret Body*, and there you mentioned that you had actually had an experience of your own that resonated quite a bit with some of the strong claims Whitley had made about, for example, having a powerful sexual experience with this female entity that he called a visitor.

Kripal: That's another reason I believe Whitley because I had a similar experience in 1989 while I was living in Calcutta, or what is now Kolkata. It happened during a Hindu tantric ritual, which made total sense in that cultural context, but it also makes really good sense in Whitley Strieber's visitor context. I could go either way, easily, but I don't believe the one any more than I believe the other. It can fit into all of these cultural contexts and mythologies almost effortlessly. That's the power of these experiences. That's also why we, I think, need to step back a bit.

Mishlove: You and Whitley are suggesting that what we need to get at is the underlying phenomenology that leads people to interpret them in terms of religion, UFO mythology, the little people, or some other form of folklore.

Kripal: Right. There may not be an underlying phenomenology. The visionary apparition might be what is appearing to us, but there is something behind or underneath that we may never be able to describe or put our finger on. I think we can still recognize that these experiences share a lot of features across cultures and times while they're also very different. This is why I'm always preaching for better forms of comparison. How do we negotiate those similarities and those differences?

Mishlove: You describe a particular methodology that is used in the humanities; it was a very elegant description of what we call hermeneutics. Let's go into that, because I've never read a better description of it than the one you put forth in that book.

Kripal: Hermeneutics is a Greek-based word based on the god Hermes, who was a trickster so that should key us off right away. Hermeneutics is the way that academics talk about interpretation. A text or an experience may not have a single correct interpretation. The text or the experience is like a living matrix of possibilities or potentials, and that when a reader or an interpreter interacts with it, a particular kind of interpretation arises between that reader and the text or the experiencer and the experience. What appears is as dependent on the interpreter as it is on what is being interpreted. There's a fusion that takes place, and that's what we mean by hermeneutics.

I think a lot of speculation about quantum physics is essentially hermeneutical. For instance, the wave function doesn't exist until the photon is observed, and then the wave function collapses. What people like Niels Bohr saw immediately, whether he was right or wrong, is that it appears that there's something about conscious observation that affects physical reality and causes the wave function to collapse and to behave in a particular way. That's a beautiful analogy for what we mean by hermeneutics. The text or the experience is like this wave function; its potential is all over the place; it's just a smear of possibilities, and the reader or the experiencer comes in and it collapses and becomes one meaning or one story or one thing.

Mishlove: I think I understand, now, why in our previous interview about Elizabeth Krohn's near-death experience, you said that we are changing the afterlife.

Kripal: The afterlife is like this quantum smear of possibilities, and we interpret it through near-death experiences. With people like Elizabeth it takes on a particular shape.

Mishlove: Speaking of the afterlife, Whitley makes a point that these experiences he's having are interwoven with what appear to be post-mortem contexts of various kinds.

Kripal: This is another time where I had a direct or indirect experience with Whitley. It involved Anne, his departed and beloved wife. I knew Anne when she was alive. When she died, Whitley asked me to come to the family ranch and do one of the readings for the memorial. It happened to be a sermon from Meister Eckhart, the great Christian medieval mystical writer and preacher.

About a year and a half later, a woman from Canada that I knew started to receive messages from Anne, and she sent them to me. She didn't know they were from Anne; instead she thought they were from Princess Leia of *Star Wars*. She sent me this drawing but I didn't recognize it. I didn't make much of it because I was absorbed in my own life and family at the time. I showed the drawing to a colleague named Diana, and she said, "Jeff, that's Anne Strieber." I was like, "Holy crap, you're right. That is Anne Strieber." I asked the artist if I could show it to Whitley. Whitley then put the drawing and a photograph of Anne side-by-side. The drawing was clearly based on the photograph, a spitting image. As I looked at the drawing more and more, I realized that the word "Anne" was written dozens of times, all through the hair, the face, and the nose.

We came to this conclusion that Anne was communicating with Whitley through this little social network that we had, and that each of us was provided a piece of the puzzle. Diana had a piece, I had a piece, this woman from Canada had a piece, and none of it would have come together without all of us. It was as if there was this séance going on across thousands of miles. The result was Whitley having a really profound, quite moving encounter with his dead wife.

Mishlove: This sounds quite reminiscent to me of what was at one time known as the cross-correspondences.

Kripal: It wasn't quite as complicated as that, but it clearly had that feel that with this particular paranormal event, there was no way to read it as just one person's private experience. It actually made no sense to the woman to whom it first appeared. It only took on meaning through this social network.

Mishlove: That was the strategy, presumably employed by Frederic Myers, whom we spoke about earlier. After his own death, it seemed as if he was attempting to establish proof of his postmortem existence by communicating through different mediums, on different continents even, and giving them pieces of a puzzle that only made sense when the pieces came together.

Kripal: I know. I thought of that when it was happening.

Mishlove: As if Anne was really trying to provide proof of her post-mortem existence.

Kripal: We were all convinced. Here, Jeffrey, I talk about the "two bars". This communication from Anne is the low bar. These experiences are why people historically have believed in an afterlife, that their loved ones survive, and why they believe there's something like a soul. Once you have an experience like this, it's really impossible not to entertain those ideas and maybe to believe them. It's clearly impossible then to think that other people are irrational or unreasonable for holding those views, because it just happened to you. You can't deny that. That's the low bar, why people believe impossible things.

    The high bar is that these impossible things are true. I actually can't get over that high bar. I can't get my readers over it. I can't get my listeners over it. I don't think it's possible, actually, to get people over that bar. But I think it's very possible to get over the low bar. I don't think we can prove it, nor is this a matter for science, but I also don't think it's pseudoscience. I don't think it has anything to do with science because it has to do with people experiencing these things, and they're not repeatable or measurable. They're certainly part of our reality. It's very easy to get over this low bar, but it's very hard and perhaps not even possible to get over the high bar.

Mishlove: I know that you wrote in your book that you don't want people to make the mistake of thinking that you believe Whitley is the equivalent of a Hebrew prophet. But when I listened to him, he came across very much in that vein, in particular with regard to his interest in ecology and in saving the planet from the destruction that humans seem to be creating. He seemed to feel that they downloaded important information that we could use to clean up the problems that we have on the planet right now. He seems so desperate to get people to listen to him on that score, and so hurt when his ideas are rejected.

Kripal: He's not like the Hebrew prophets in the sense that we no longer have a recognized institution of prophecy in our culture.

Mishlove: That's for sure.

Kripal: The ancient Israelites seemed to have institutionalized this notion of prophecy. Some of the greatest Hebrew prophets were actually employed at the court, literally working for the king. We don't have a prophet in the president's cabinet, to put it mildly. What I did say in this book, which I am completely convinced of, is that Whitley is an American shaman, which is an indigenous way of calling him a prophet, but he lives in a culture in which there are no shamans.

I think this is why Whitley suffers so. He has these gifts and access to the other world, which is constantly speaking to him. He has messages for our public culture, but our public culture does not recognize that other world, or the role of the shaman or prophet. Whitley comes across to people as just another crazy person because we lack utterly any cultural context for what this man is experiencing.

Mishlove: One of the reasons I take Whitley very seriously is because many of his experiences are reminiscent of what

I uncovered in a 10-year case study I did with Ted Owens—who called himself the PK man—and had similar experiences as those reported by Whitley. Like Whitley, he worked throughout his life to interest scientists in what he had done and produced many, many demonstrations that seemed to be evidence of psychokinetic abilities or perhaps even a telepathic connection with some sort of extraterrestrial or hyperdimensional beings.

Kripal: I love the book *PK Man*, Jeff. It sits here in my office, right on my desk, so I can tempt people with it. It has a very cool cover, too, by the way. I think that's a really powerful comparison. In the book I wrote with Elizabeth Krohn, *Changed in a Flash,* I have a whole section on lightning lore. This notion of getting hit by lightning and becoming a visionary or a shaman is very distributed and very old as well.

I think you're right. With the Ted Owens case, there again, you have this really weird mix of something mental and something very, very physical; in this case, atmospheric.

Mishlove: I suppose the unique feature of Whitley's experience is that, in effect, it began with a rape. He explained to me that he still suffers the physical consequences of having some sort of an instrument inserted into his rectum.

Kripal: Yeah. And again, that's not unique either. Physical trauma, sexual abuse, wartime trauma, emotional trauma, is the origin of a lot of saints, prophets, and visionary figures. There's something about trauma that cracks people open and maims us forever. I have a whole chapter in the book on trauma. It's a horrible thing and I don't want to romanticize it in any way, but some people later develop these gifts or abilities. I don't know if Elizabeth Krohn talked to you about this, but she traces her near-death experience not just back to the lightning strike, but to six years of being sexually abused as a little girl.

Mishlove: Oh, yes. Of course, we talked about that.

Kripal: And I don't mean an adolescent or a teenager. I mean a little girl. This poor thing was raped, essentially, for six years. She learned to dissociate.

Mishlove: Between the ages of six and 12, as I recall.

Kripal: Elizabeth is just adamant that that ability to dissociate is what allowed her to survive the lightning strike.

Mishlove: In your chapter, you relate trauma to trance.

Kripal: Yes, and to transcendence. I really believe that and Whitley is just as clear about this. He has always, as far back as I can remember reading—maybe not in *Communion*, but certainly in the books after that—traced his visitor experiences back to childhood trauma that occurred on a military base. He could never remember what the abuse or trauma was, but he has always been really clear about that. He never says that the visitors are just psychic projections of this earlier trauma. He thinks the trauma split him open in some way, and it allowed the visitors access to him later in his life. That's a different argument.

Mishlove: It also seems in Whitley's experience that he is being taken possession of; that these beings really want to control him; that they raped him as a way of breaking his spirit. And now he loves them. He almost worships these experiences, in spite of all of the pain and discomfort. He describes it in the most positive terms, with the biggest smile on his face. It makes him happy in a way that nothing else seems to do, especially since the death of his wife.

Kripal: That's right. I discuss this notion in the book, *The Supernatural*, that the sacred is both terrifying, dangerous, and filled with awe and beauty. That's how humans have responded to this presence for as long as we can see back. The holy is not the good. The holy is the powerful and the awesome.

Mishlove: It seems as if humans are always fascinated with power, and wish to accumulate more and more power, that we're drawn to it.

Kripal: It's like touching the light socket. Do you really want to put a fork in the outlet? And you know, you do. How much power can you take? One of my guilty memories as a child was convincing my little brother to touch the electric fence on our grandma and grandpa's farm with a steel rod. That's not going to kill you, but it's really going to shock the heck out of you. There's something awesome about that experience, but there's also something bad about it.

Mishlove: Most people, if they've had one experience like that, they don't go back for a second one. But Whitley seems to be different in that regard.

Kripal: I don't think that his experiences are touching the electric fence. I think they have this ecstatic, and frankly, aesthetic quality to them that draws him back.

Mishlove: I, personally, am fascinated by the ostensibly concrete physical aspects of this. He went into some length with me about the incident where the implant was supposedly put into his ear and what happened to the alarm system in his house at the time. The garage door was opened, but the alarm didn't go off. A worker came and found an unusual magnetic field there that apparently interfered with the alarm system, but they couldn't find any source for the magnetic field. It certainly suggests that a diligent scientist could study him and come up with some really concrete findings.

Kripal: Maybe. That's the point in our book together where I feel like I really failed. That story about the implant is in our book, and he's told it elsewhere. I didn't know what to do with that story, because it implies that there are human beings who are intentionally doing this to other human beings under cover of darkness, as it were. I stumble in the book, and point out that getting objects implanted in the body is an old shamanic motif, too. Maybe this was more of a visionary experience that Whitley translated into modern conspiracy terms. That feels like something of a cop-out to me, looking back on it. I don't know what to do with that, Jeffrey. I'm just kind of at a loss.

Mishlove: You are a religious scholar, not a para-physicist. However, it seems to me that in the religious literature there are various examples, I think, in the life of Abraham and the Hebrew Torah, where angels of God come, but they appear like humans.

Kripal: You're right. I do think there's something very physical or even electromagnetic about these events. Again, I'm not a physicist or an electrician, so I wouldn't even know how to begin to study those things.

Mishlove: But you did speculate in your book that we may have a—I think the way you put it is that we may have a soul which is like a luminous plasma.

Kripal: That's Whitley's idea, and it sounds reasonable to me. Elizabeth sees auras around the human body. There's nothing really that outrageous about positing some kind of electromagnetic dimension to the human being. The heart is basically an electrical system. Clearly there is electromagnetic stuff going on.

This reminds me of a story. David Hufford, who's a friend of mine, wrote a wonderful book called *The Terror That Comes in the Night*. He's studied sleep paralysis, among other things. David is of the conviction that some sleep paralysis events cannot be explained away, and that there do appear to be some entities that interact with humans during these events.

He also wrote this book *The World Was Flooded with Light: A Mystical Experience Remembered* with Genevieve Foster who had this massive mystical opening in which the world became light for days. I remember asking David about what that meant. What do we mean when we say, "I saw the light?" Is this the same thing as photons and me turning on a light bulb? David said, "I asked Genevieve whether she could read a newspaper by this light that she saw for days. She said no." That to me is a really significant hint. It doesn't mean the light wasn't there or there is no such light. It means we're probably talking about a light that is not what the physicists are talking about with photons.

Mishlove: I understand that perfectly well, because I experience tinnitus from time to time. It's a very distinct sound. I can hear it as if there were a bell ringing in the room, but I know nobody else can hear it but me.

Kripal: Yeah. It's your eardrum, right?

Mishlove: I'm not quite sure where it's produced. I assume somewhere in the brain.

Kripal: What is the nature of this? Is it electromagnetic or is it some other kind of exotic energy or life force that we just don't have language for? I don't know, of course.

Mishlove: You do write about other instances, for example, when people see these glowing orbs. It's not just the experience of seeing a strange light hovering in the room or in the garden near you. It often involves an experience of ecstasy.

Kripal: You could write a whole history about orbs of light in religious texts. That's kind of what the history of religions is, right? From St. Paul to the burning bush. They have a subjective component and they have an objective component and those two things are resonating, working off each other.

Mishlove: And, of course, the deeper metaphysical question that you're getting at in your work with Whitley, and what strikes me when you talk about a new vision of the unexplained, is that consciousness itself is capable of manifesting or creating phenomena in the physical world. That's basically what we call psychokinesis. That may be much more widespread than we realize.

Kripal: If you want to take that further, maybe the physical world is a manifestation of consciousness. That's what a lot of these figures would say. That's what we call idealism. I think that's on the table here.

Mishlove: Certainly our mutual friend Bernardo Kastrup has gone a long way to articulate in very precise language the argument for the idealist position.

Kripal: I'm very sympathetic to that. What you end up concluding if you look at this stuff long enough or you interact with it closely enough—and most people can't, of course, I understand—is that consciousness is not just something going on in your brain. It's somehow interwoven into the physical universe all around you as well. It's as basic and fundamental as gravity. But what that means, I don't know.

Mishlove: You conclude the book with a very interesting metaphor. You suggest that perhaps we are like the fictional characters in a movie, but we're also the author of the movie at the same time.

Kripal: That I actually do believe. That was the basic idea of the *Authors of the Impossible Book*, that we're writing this stuff, but also experiencing it. That was the argument in the book with Elizabeth, too, that we're scripting these things, but not individually. We're scripting them as cultures and families and generations, and then our descendants experience the world in these terms. They think it's somehow external or objective, but we wrote it. Again, that doesn't mean it's a series of fictions, because the author is quite real. We just haven't turned around to see the author.

Mishlove: There's a fundamental paradox there in the nature of reality itself, that we think the subjective and the objective are two distinct things, but they're not.

Kripal: That would be my position.

Mishlove: Professor Jeffrey Kripal, once again, this has been a real pleasure to have a conversation about a topic that, as you point out, not everybody has the privilege of being able to think about. I get a lot of feedback from our viewers that they're very grateful to be able to share in these conversations, and I'm very grateful that you were able to create the time for it as well.

Kripal: It is a privilege, Jeffrey, and none of us could do this without the people who have these experiences. Those are the real heroes here, not the geeks or the nerds or the scientists trying to figure it out. We're doing our best, but the gifts actually lie with the experiencers, and that's where I feel nothing but awe, humility, and confusion, frankly.

Mishlove: I have to say I experienced all of those myself interacting with Whitley, but I'm hoping to have him come to Albuquerque so we can do more.

Kripal: He'd be great at that. You might want to think twice about rooming with him!

9

Ingo Swann's *Penetration*
with
Daz Smith

~

Jeffrey Mishlove: Today we're going to explore Ingo Swann's [1933-2013] mysterious book *Penetration*. Many of you will know that Ingo Swann is often regarded as the father of remote viewing. His book, *Penetration*, has to do with the mystery of UFOs. There are many other facets of Ingo Swann's remarkable life related to UFOs. My guest today is Daz Smith. He is the publisher of the *Eight Martinis* magazine for the remote viewing community. He is also author of several books including: *Surfing the Psychic Internet, Remote Viewing Dialogues, CRV: Controlled Remote Viewing,* and *Remote Viewing 9/11.* Daz is based in the United Kingdom. Welcome, Daz. It's a pleasure to be with you today.

Daz Smith: Thanks for having me along. It's great to be here. I'm a great admirer of your work.

Mishlove: We're going to be talking about Ingo Swann today. I've done other programs about Ingo Swann. I know he's somebody you met with personally. For those who may not be familiar with Ingo it would be fair to say that he's almost universally regarded as the father of remote viewing, even though that might be somewhat misleading.

Smith: If you asked him this question he always said the real father was Harold Puthoff, his co-founder. But, yes, he's known around the world as the father of remote viewing.

Mishlove: To me remote viewing is simply what we used to call free response clairvoyance. That's been around for many decades before Ingo Swann, Hal Puthoff, the team at SRI and SAIC came on the scene.

Smith: I think what Ingo added was that we should practice what we were doing within the scientific protocol. That's what makes remote viewing different from what I call the classical techniques.

Mishlove: You've been involved in remote viewing now yourself for several decades.

Smith: Yes, 24 years going on 25 years as we speak, practicing pretty much every day, definitely every week, and for the last four years, one of the very few full-time paid remote viewers as well.

Mishlove: Which is very impressive. I know you're working in the area of forecasting financial trends, particularly in the bitcoin market.

Smith: We do gold markets as well and the other markets, such as the S&P 500 and stuff, but generally cryptos and news predictions as well.

Mishlove: You also had the pleasure of visiting Ingo Swann at his home in New York City.

Smith: In 2011 Ingo invited me to stay for a week. I only stayed for the day because he was getting quite ill at that point. But it was a magical experience walking into Ingo's home and then being surrounded by his artwork, all his files, and books. That was a pretty amazing experience for someone like me who has been engrossed in and really interested in this subject for over two decades.

Mishlove: You had hundreds of questions that you wanted to ask Ingo. I imagine you did ask as many as you could in the time that you had.

Smith: We covered all subjects. I wanted to ask quite a lot of questions about the history of Controlled Remote Viewing (CRV) and Remote Viewing (RV) because it's still quite fragmented. I spent many years trying to piece that together through freedom of information documents. I also wanted to ask him questions related to the latest article that I just put out, about his book *Penetration,* and his alleged remote viewing of the moon for intelligence agencies.

Mishlove: Ingo is really famous for having used remote viewing to visit the moon, Jupiter, Mercury, I think, Mars—prior to the various NASA space probes—and for the accurate information about those planets that was not known by the astronomical community at the time.

Smith: Ingo did some great explorative work. Not enough like that is done using remote viewing today. I'm hoping to reignite that. He started off with Jupiter in 1973 and moved on to Mercury in 1974, the moon in 1975; then he went back to Mars four times in 1975, and in 1976, twice. Then he went back in 1984 with a larger project with his best CRV student, Tom McNear. That was a pretty spectacular project that Tom recently presented at IRVA [International Remote Viewing Association] this year.

Mishlove: It was well known that Ingo was able to use remote viewing, or what some people then were calling traveling clairvoyance, to visit other planets and to accurately describe publicly available technical details about those planets.

Smith: Ingo did some great work, for example, describing things on Jupiter that hadn't been scientifically considered before he described them. The University of West Georgia archives is putting Ingo Swann's old files online. There's a very detailed report in there of all of Ingo's observations. It's really interesting because he explored it before any probes had gone there. Over the years, as he gathered more evidence and feedback, he color-coded it in this document. It's really exciting to see in his own hand.

Mishlove: I'm pretty sure that one of the findings he came up with was the idea that there were rings around Jupiter.

Smith: Yes, he did.

Mishlove: His book, *Penetration,* which we'll be talking about, is very mysterious to most people. Not that there's anything mysterious in the book itself, it's very straightforward, but the phenomenon that he claims he observed and reports on in that book seems so out of the ordinary, one might even say bizarre, that I think many people including myself have a hard time believing it, and at the same time, a hard time disbelieving it.

Smith: When I was face to face with Ingo I asked him questions about that book and one of them was that very question. I literally said, "When you read the book it does read like a fantastical story and a lot of people find it hard to believe." He straight faced me. The entire time he sat there, he was puffing on his big cigar. He bent forward and he looked me straight in the eye and he said, "If *you* think it's fantastic, how do you think it felt for me going through the entire process?" He left me with no other idea of the situation. It was all a genuine experience for him.

Mishlove: We'll talk about it in some detail but before we get into it I think it's fair to say that the people who knew Ingo intimately, who studied Ingo's remarkable clairvoyant abilities, who were his students and friends, have all acknowledged that this man was a straight shooter. He was not the type of person to fabricate a story.

Smith: I asked as many friends and colleagues of his that I could find. I even tracked down some colleagues that a lot of people didn't know about. I spoke with really close friends of Ingo's who worked on the same projects as well as the *Penetration* people. Everyone to a "T" said—and I know this from meeting him as well—he wasn't the kind of person to make things up or to lie or even exaggerate things.

Mishlove: He worked very closely with scientists. Let's talk about the story itself that Ingo tells in this book.

Smith: Essentially, Ingo details that, while he was working at SRI, he was approached by a man he calls Mr. Axelrod, obviously a pseudonym. Axelrod had some very strange bodyguards who looked like "special forces" twins. They took him on several trips to an underground facility. Ingo was blindfolded but, over time, he thought it might have been somewhere in Alaska, just from some of the things that happened on the trip. While he was there, he was asked to remote view locations on the moon. Ingo then described very strange structures on the moon. Later on as well in the book Ingo details how they also took him on a trip to a location—again he feels it was in Alaska—where he saw a UFO shaped craft materialize.

Mishlove: If I remember correctly, it sort of came out of a lake.

Smith: Yes, that's correct. It was quite a dangerous situation, or appeared to be so in the book, because Ingo said that it noticed that they were watching so they had to run through the forest to escape.

Mishlove: In other words, this object—we'll call it a UFO— was attacking them.

Smith: It seemed to be the case. That's what Ingo seems to indicate in the book. Yes, absolutely.

Mishlove: He even claims he was injured.

Smith: Yes. He details that he was running for the woods, and he wasn't a very athletic person at this time, and he did injure himself.

Mishlove: In other words, the gist of the story is that there's some sort of a secret organization, it's not even clear who they are, but they seem to know a lot about UFO activity right here on this planet. They were able to bring Ingo to a remote location, a lake somewhere in the northern woods, probably Alaska, where he witnessed a UFO, you say materializing, but as I recall it sort of rose out of the water from a lake.

Smith: It's not that fantastical nowadays if people do research into the UFO field because it's a pretty common story. UFOs are frequently reported near big bodies of water. We have had, for the last couple of years, the infamous Nimitz Tic Tac UFO event video as well. In the latest piece of footage we see one of those UFOs descending under the surface of the water.

Mishlove: In your new issue of *Eight Martinis* you go into Ingo's exploration of potential ET contacts on the earth. You include, for example, an old 1992 article that Ingo wrote for *Fate Magazine*. He implies that these aliens are obviously very psychic. Every time an abduction or a contact experience is reported, the bewildered people who come out of these experiences say, "They communicated with me telepathically." He wonders, why is it that they seem to be so psychic and in our human culture there seems to be a large-scale effort all across the planet to suppress psychic functioning, to deny that it even exists. He wonders if the aliens aren't the ones behind this, that they don't want us to develop abilities to the same degree that they have. He's urging readers of his article to move beyond that, to develop what he called the ability to penetrate the UFO enigma.

Smith: He goes into detail on it under a heading called "Psychic castration." He details how this has gone on probably for centuries. In part, we've done it to ourselves but maybe we've been guided in that process. In Europe we had the witch trials. Anyone who showed any intuitive ability was burned at the stake or suffered a horrible death. Right now we have religions that are holding intuitive people back, and larger society is also to a degree. There may be—I like to call it non-human because we don't know what they are yet—presence that seems to be manipulating us, especially when they have contacts with humans which we call abductions nowadays.

Mishlove: Ingo seemed to be quite convinced back in 1992 that the alien presence has been on Earth for a very long time and that we were probably the result of a genetic engineering program conducted by these non-humans going back maybe 50,000 years or so. He also suggests that they have a mining operation on the moon.

Smith: We know the moon is rich in all kinds of minerals and materials so that makes great sense. Again, going back to the dawn of telescopes and astronomers, we have reports of lights and all kinds of activity on the moon. I've been looking at this whole moon-Mars situation with remote viewing for over two decades. I can count literally hundreds of remote viewers under many different circumstances and blind conditions, who report that both the moon and Mars have structures and activity, which seem to indicate mining and other facilities.

Mishlove: I thought it was very interesting that you published two articles by Ingo that came out in *Fate* magazine. In 1992, he's urging the readers to join him in a new movement to penetrate the alien enigma and to find out through remote viewing what these aliens are really up to. Then, in the second article he goes on a different tack, it seems to me. He's suggesting that if you do remote viewing without physical feedback so you know whether your vision under remote viewing is accurate or not, you're not really doing remote viewing at all; you're deviating from the scientific protocol.

Obviously, that would apply to almost all efforts to penetrate the UFO enigma through remote viewing.

Smith: He does remark in the same article that he's part of this situation as well because he's been doing these experiments. It's an enigma and, as we know from articles after this, Ingo did what I would call "non-blind remote viewing" and remote viewing of these areas like the moon with no physical feedback. It's very contradictory what he's saying there. But I can understand why he's saying it like that. If you're someone like Ingo for example, he did over a million experiments in scientific conditions, so he has a very established track record of accuracy that you can use as a gauge even if he's going a bit in left field and doing a front loaded, what I would call an esoteric type target.

Mishlove: Let's talk about what front loading means for the benefit of those who don't know that term.

Smith: The majority of remote viewing is done blind. There's usually a tasker that's in another location from a remote viewer and they set up a task. They might write down on a sheet of paper or type into their computer, "I want Daz to visit the moon." Then they'll assign that a random number. All we get as the remote viewer is the random number. We know nothing about the target up front. With some of the work that Ingo did, for example from the transcript we found from 1999, Ingo knew that he would be remote viewing the moon to look for something. He was what we call "front loaded" in that regard. He wasn't blinded anymore.

Mishlove: The problem with front loading is that once the ego, the intellect, gets involved it will develop all sorts of scenarios and fantasies and strategies because the intellect tries to figure all this out logically.

Smith: Most people wouldn't believe this if they're not practicing remote viewers, but knowing about the target, front loading, actually makes it a lot harder to assess the target. The mind tries to guess what the target is, based on that sliver of information. So most of us as remote viewers hate front loading. Although, I've worked 250 missing person cases for different police forces in the United States. It's good to know I'm working a missing person case, because it then allows me to tailor my RV information so that I describe more locational details. All the police want to know is the location. Front loading can be good for operational use but it's a very fine balance between how much information is too much.

Mishlove: Let's talk about Ingo's visits to the moon. You found detailed information in the files. I think you've talked to Ingo's partner in some of these adventures, Bob Durant, so you have quite a bit of information about it, with the caveat that it potentially might all be fantasy.

Smith: As with most of the RV session data that I've seen over the years regarding the moon—I've collected quite a lot—we do not have sufficient feedback yet to verify the data. All we can say is a lot of people and a lot of scientists report anomalous phenomena on the moon. Someone like me may have a very good accuracy level that you can take into account but, until we get proper feedback, and I don't know when that may be coming, you have to take all the RV data with a pinch of salt, I believe.

Mishlove: Ingo had these adventures. Let's begin by describing them.

Smith: It's quite a complex situation because in the mid-1990s, Ingo Swann made friends and teamed up with a quite prominent UFO researcher, at the time, called Bob Durant. I think Ingo did have a bit of an interest before that but, when they got together, Bob was the catalyst that really made Ingo look at the ET or non-human intelligence phenomena bit more with his RV. From the letters and communications in the Ingo Swann archives going back and forth between Bob and Ingo you can see this friendship really develop and blossom. Ingo also reached out to people in his local area. He went to some of the UFO meetings and gave talks in New Jersey to local UFO groups.

Bob and Ingo met a person named Richard Butler. I don't have many details on Richard Butler other than he was another UFO researcher working in the New York area in the mid 1990s. There are some notes that he might have been a UFO abductee or experiencer, but he was a client. He took some files when Ingo died saying they were his. He paid for Bob and several others to work on several projects collectively called the *Luna-Mares Project* looking at locations on and above the moon. I only have details of one of them. I've had many conversations with Richard Butler and some of them are detailed in the article but he's very reluctant to release a lot of the information because he indicates that there are people telling him that he's not allowed to release it.

Mishlove: That adds to the mystery, I suppose. In reading through the material one of the phrases that kept coming up was DOMA. It suggests that DOMA represents a particular organization or group of non-humans who are functioning on the moon. I also gather there's something feminine about DOMA.

Smith: Yes. DOMA stands for the Daughters of Ma. Richard Butler, and I guess Ingo and Bob Durant came to believe this as well that there are a group of extraterrestrial women that are organizing and controlling, at some level, everything in our local universe. Richard claims that they're working with our governments. They're also connected to us through our DNA like they manipulated us in some way—we're their ancestors. (*sic*) It's very strange. Like most things, I have no information to back any of this up. All I can say is Ingo and Bob seemed to believe it. They took the lead from this and this led them to go back to the moon. They detail it in the letters and in the documents, that DOMA gave Ingo an invitation to go to the moon and commune with them.

Mishlove: I know all of this seems very fantastical, but I can say from my own experience, working in comparable situations doing remote viewing of this sort with groups of people, that oftentimes these scenarios, that seem to be fantasy, turn out to be verifiable.

Smith: Hopefully one day this will, too. It's really interesting stuff. One good thing about it is that we have this remote viewing transcript now. What I'm hoping, over the next few years—because we have the coordinates that Ingo used for the moon as well—is that myself and some other people that are interested and dedicated enough might do further research to take this to another level. We shall see.

Mishlove: What you found are actual audio tapes that have been transcribed, of Ingo reporting in real time what he is experiencing when his clairvoyant body or his astral body or his consciousness, is on the moon. He expects that he's been invited there by this ET organization known as DOMA, the Daughters of Ma, but when he gets there, if I recall correctly, they kick him out.

Smith: They kick him out on his very first visit by what he called a male telepath. I think that angered Ingo somewhat and that's why he came back for this transcript that we have because he ends up summoning the being that originally kicked him out. They have quite an in-depth conversation, which is very interesting.

Mishlove: He's beginning to, at least in his own mind, learn about what this DOMA organization is about.

Smith: Yes. They say they've been around for something like forty-thousand years and they're on an exodus through the solar system in this huge mothership. What's quite interesting as well, there's an illustration called MS15 on the page with the transcript that used to be on Ingo Swann's website when it was up originally. It was essentially a clue that Ingo hid in his original website hoping that a remote viewer would see that image. Essentially, it's a sketch of the solar system but around one of the planets there is an object that he called MS-15. I found out some details about this after Ingo died. During a project Ingo did many years ago, he viewed the far reaches of the universe and some of the planets. He said he found a huge mothership orbiting one of the planets. He was hoping other remote viewers might find this hint and they would also remote view it and send him information. But as I'm aware of today no one actually hit the target or sent the right information in.

Mishlove: Where do you think things ended up? Ingo died in 2013 a couple of years after you visited him in 2011. Do you have any sense of Ingo's final appraisal of this human/non-human interaction?

Smith: No, this article is as far as I've got, though I do know there's more. We do know that after Ingo passed, Richard Butler, the person that was the client for the *Luna-Mares* projects, went to Ingo's house and spoke with Ellie, who is Ingo's niece and executor. He took all those files. I also know that Bob Durant, who passed not long after Ingo, had some files as well. I've been tracking down Bob's files and have found some. There's another remote viewer who has a copy of those files and he might even have the audio tapes for these transcripts as well as other audio tapes. I'm still trying to put the pieces of the puzzle together and I don't have a full picture at this stage other than I'm very aware that Ingo did many explorations. I have details about a big Roswell crash file that they had. The evidence was so compelling that they tried to get the UFO and Roswell researchers at the time to look at the data and to give them some feedback on it but they were unsuccessful. Bob Durant then made his own Roswell documentary in the early 1990s. There's lots of stuff there but nothing conclusive.

Mishlove: As I recall, Bob Durant's documentary about Roswell was praised by Steven Spielberg.

Smith: Yes. Great praise that is. I think he said it's one of the best documentaries, at that time, he'd seen on Roswell.

Mishlove: I think it's fair to say that the entire remote viewing community developed a fascination with UFOs going at least as far back as the 1990s, if not earlier.

Smith: There's so much evidence coming out about this now. It's a very interesting time to be alive. I think we're seeing a big convergence of what we're doing with remote viewing, telepathy, and other types of psychic skills and that governments are admitting that there's definitely something going on with non-human intelligences.

Mishlove: It's very interesting. Ingo, in his 1992 article, was really complaining, and I think in the 1993 article as well, that the UFO researchers in general don't want to have anything to do with the psychic aspects. Parapsychologists, in general, don't want to have anything to do with the UFO enigma. It's as if these two areas of, you could call it parascience, are both so threatened, struggling so hard to achieve a level of respectability and inroads into the establishment that they're afraid to deal with each other. Ingo seemed to feel that this is holding everything back.

Smith: It was pretty bad in the 1980s and the 1990s. I believe things have changed now. A lot of the top UFO researchers out there are using the services of remote viewers to aid in their research. I know Linda Moulton Howe, for example, has used many remote viewers including Joe McMoneagle on projects. The funny thing is, in the 1980s and onwards, remote viewing had a lot of credibility because of its 20-year Stargate history, whereas UFOs had a really bad day in the press. Anyone who said they were into UFOs was looked at as a kook.

It has turned on its head now because of the 'Tic Tac' Nimitz data. UFOs have become really acceptable nowadays. The UFO researchers and the people that are looking at UFOs don't like remote viewing to be communicated in the same terms as what is now the new term "UAPs." They feel that their topic is more credible whereas remote viewing isn't. So the tables have turned but there are UFO and remote viewing people working together. There are people, such as Steven Greer, who call what they're doing CE5 remote viewing. I don't think it's remote viewing but he is trying to communicate with non-human intelligences in an intuitive manner. That's getting a lot of traction as well, so lots is happening out there.

Mishlove: My own philosophy, Daz, is that the human race is not going to enter the galactic community of interstellar travelers until we are able to master our own minds, until we can plumb the depths of parapsychology, until we understand the connection between the afterlife and the alien community, because there are many examples of aliens and deceased humans appearing together in various abduction accounts. What do you think of that?

Smith: For 25 years I've tried to work out what's happening there. I started with UFO research before I looked at remote viewing. Before I looked at UFO research, I spent many years looking at what I call classical psychic techniques, such as clairvoyance, mediumship, healing, Tarot readings and all that kind of stuff. I have to say, the more I look at all of it, the more confounded I am by what I'm finding. It was once described to me in a non-human communication during a channeling session that there is an entire universe that we're looking at, and Earth is at the center of this giant onion that has all these layers. In each layer of this giant onion there are these different entities trying to communicate. There's lots of shades of gray here. Some of these entities have different intentions for us than we would like but some of them have beautiful intentions for us.

Mishlove: In other words, the situation is so complex that we have a hard time even finding words for it.

Smith: That is true through all of the psychic experiences I've ever had. When you have a true psychic experience and then you try to communicate that to someone in words and pictures you can only do half the job. I think that's the issue the entities have with us. They're trying to communicate the wonderful vastness and beauty of all this and there just aren't words for it, really. After twenty-four years of doing pure remote viewing, I've concluded that there's a force or a living entity of some kind behind the remote viewing process. Every time I, or people I know, feel like they've got somewhere, we've got it down pat, and we know the answers, the very next day it's turned on its head. It's almost like there's this trickster in the universe that likes to keep us guessing, like we're just not ready yet to know the answers that we're seeking.

Mishlove: A lot of the work you're doing—we touched on it briefly regarding the area of financial forecasting—is similar to my way of thinking. I've engaged in financial forecasting. The markets are intelligent. When you begin to find a pattern or find a way of predicting future trends, the markets will adjust to that. Anytime you think you've got a handle on the markets, the markets have a handle on you. I think the same thing is true with the ET situation and looking out at the universe in general. It's intelligent. It knows that we're watching.

Smith: I've been targeted on many blinded UFO type projects myself. For example, one that I did for the Farsight Institute was a blind remote viewing of the Phoenix lights incident that happened in the 1990s. This massive triangle-shaped craft hovered over the city of Phoenix for several hours and was photographed and videoed from different points all over the city. While I was doing a remote viewing session of that incident years later, trying to penetrate the craft and look around inside to get a feel for it, I and the other remote viewers on the team did have a dialogue with the non-humans in that craft. This happens all the time. It's very hard to communicate to other people the type of experience you have with these entities. It's hard enough for them to communicate with humans what they're experiencing and what they're trying to do. Then we try to get that through the very small bandwidth of human consciousness down onto a sheet of paper, which makes it even harder. But I have to say, it's an amazing and beautiful thing to be involved with.

Mishlove: I'm under the impression that Ingo himself was very much leaning towards the work of Zecharia Sitchin and other writers who talk about non-humans having a very ancient influence on the development of human civilization. If I recall correctly, Sitchin suggests that we were originally created through genetic engineering to be used as a race of slaves to engage in mining operations on behalf of these extraterrestrials, if that's actually the case. But it would seem that whether or not they were using humans as slaves, that ended a long time ago. The human race has evolved a great deal since then. Maybe we're evolving to a point where we can think of these vastly superior creative beings, at least at some level, as our equals.

Smith: I'm not sure we're their equals at this stage because if so then there wouldn't be abduction events. I feel that abduction is negative. But, at the same time, field biologists consider it helping animals in the wild that are having a problem by tranquilizing them. So, it's a hard situation, and I don't really understand what's going on with it. I'm not sure Ingo did as well from all the files that I've read. I feel his viewpoint flip-flopped over the years. His early 1992 and 1993 articles are vastly different from his experiences that he had in 1999 when he went back to the moon for the final time and had these conversations. It's a very complex situation.

I also believe that we're probably talking about a multitude of different non-humans here as well. We may look at things in black and white and think about non-humans as the grays or the tall nordic looking ones, but I think it's vastly more complex than that. At the same time, I still believe it's a beautiful thing and we are on the cusp with the revelations that are coming out. I know there are more revelations because I've been talking to and been remote viewing for some of the people that are involved in the disclosure. It's going to be a very interesting time over the next three or four years, I believe.

Mishlove: You mentioned that you worked with the Farsight Institute. Of course, the Farsight Institute was involved in a scandal in which they reported certain observations they believed to be true. It led other people, who learned of their reports, to commit one of those horrible mass suicides many years ago. I think it serves as a warning for people to be cautious about how they interpret these remote viewing events.

Smith: With all the projects I do for people I have a caveat: be wary of the information. They should only use remote viewing information in connection with other forms of information. There should always be feedback for the projects as well. The Farsight project you're referring to was the Hale-Bopp incident back in the late 1990s. I've spoken to Courtney Brown from Farsight about that many times. He seems to believe that, because they were in a volatile time when remote viewing was just becoming public, that they were duped and it was some kind of intelligence campaign to make Farsight look bad. I don't know about this though I've tried to find out what had happened. I also spoke to the people involved at Heaven's Gate about the mass suicide and about the effect remote viewing might have had. They made it absolutely clear to me that, for at least a decade before the Farsight predictions of the Hale-Bopp comet, they had already made up their mind that they were going to leave the planet by mass suicide. They assured me that the remote viewing of Hale-Bopp had no influence on their decision.

Mishlove: Thank you for informing me and our viewers about that little piece of information. It sheds a completely different light on a very troubling episode. Daz, I'm very delighted to have had this conversation with you. I know that your knowledge of remote viewing is incredibly vast. You've been publishing about it now for a long time. I look forward to having future conversations. I'm sure there's a great deal more that we can explore.

Smith: It has been fantastic. I admire the work you're doing. Your videos are some of the best video resources on YouTube and on the Internet, so thank you for having me.

10

UFOs and the United States Government
with
Greg Bishop

J**effrey Mishlove:** Hello and welcome. I'm Jeffrey Mishlove. Our topic today is the US Government and UFOs. I'm with Greg Bishop, who is the author of *Project Beta: The Story of Paul Bennewitz, National Security, and the Creation of a Modern UFO Myth.* He is also co-author of *"A" is For Adamsky,* an encyclopedic book about UFO contactees, and another title called *It Defies Language,* a collection of his essays about UFOs and the UFO community. Welcome, Greg.

Greg Bishop: Thanks for having me.

Mishlove: It's a pleasure to meet you, and a pleasure to be with you.

Bishop: Yes. I've been listening to and watching your show for years, and I never thought I'd actually be on it, much less in the studio with you. So, this is wonderful.

Mishlove: Let's begin by addressing your long-standing interest in ufology.

Bishop: Most people say that it was an incident or a sighting or something that happened to them. I just read all the books in the library when I was a child about UFOs, the paranormal, Bigfoot and the Loch Ness monster. For some reason, I was fascinated with that stuff. I have no idea why. That interest followed me into adulthood. When that happens, you really start getting specialized. It seems like the UFO thing captured my imagination more than the other ones. But of course, I'm still interested in those things. And there's so many connections between them.

Mishlove: I suspect most of us are unfamiliar with the Paul Bennewitz case, which is our focus today. We're going to look at your book, *Project Beta*. Let's begin by talking about who Paul Bennewitz was; why this case is so crucial in our understanding of the history of the field of ufology. A good starting point is that it occurred in Albuquerque.

Bishop: There's a huge research facility here called Kirtland Air Force Base. It is a center of satellite technology and development of weapons systems, everything. There are a lot of black projects that go on at Kirtland Air Force Base under various different authorities. Some of them are concerned with the security of these projects and that's what Paul Bennewitz ran into when he started watching lights taking off, in the middle of the night, from his porch. His wife still lives in their house that overlooks Kirtland Air Force Base.

He started seeing lights in the middle of the night in the winter, just lifting up off the ground and flying over and behind Manzano Mountain weapons storage facility. He started videotaping these lights. Since he was a UFO researcher and a member of the Aerial Phenomena Research Organization [APRO], which was a huge civilian UFO research organization in the 1950s and 1960s, he started to develop the idea that these were UFOs or alien craft. He felt like he really had to tell the people on the base.

He started a company, Thunder Scientific, which still makes measuring instruments—I think it's temperature and humidity instruments—for various different entities, including the government. He thought it was his patriotic duty to inform the base authorities about the lights. So, he wrote to people at the base, specifically the security people, Air Force Office of Special Investigations, which is kind of like the Air Force's FBI, and other people like the NSA and CIA who had presence there, and still do. They thought, "Who is this? Why is he looking at these things? And why is he saying these things?" They don't know who he is; they don't know what his interest is, and he's talking about aliens.

Mishlove: But wasn't he already involved as a contractor with the base? They knew him in that context?

Bishop: I've not been able to find out if he had a specific contract with the base, but he did have specific contracts with government entities to provide these measuring instruments. He was an electrical engineer—I think he had a master's in electrical engineering—and was very good mechanically and at building things. He built his own computers and wrote the software for them back in the mid to late 1970s, when you couldn't even buy a computer. He was really good at what he did.

But his Achilles heel, if you want to say that's what it was, was his interest in UFOs and his ability to, as Bill Moore told me, make leaps of logic based on incomplete information. He wrote to the Air Force base security and said, "I really need to tell you about this." They thought, "I guess we'd better meet with him to see what he wants to say." He went to the base and they had a meeting. I was told by an NSA person I talked to that there were about ten to fifteen people there but by the end of the meeting, there were only two people left. People left saying, "This has nothing to do with us. We don't have to worry about this." And they just took off.

The only people left, I believe, were Richard Doty and perhaps Ernest Edwards, who were with the Air Force Office of Special Investigations. They told him, "Yes, Paul, we're very interested in what you have. Please keep telling us more." They didn't tell them to stop. People ask me that, "Why didn't they just tell them to stop looking at these things and talking about them? Just like, please be quiet. These are black projects." The reason was that when something like this happens, intelligence agencies want to know why the person is doing what they're doing. More importantly, who might be listening to him? Who's talking to him? How do we trace these relationships with people that are not UFO people but really are interested in what's going on the base? Intelligence agencies all over the world gather information and they collate it into a picture about what the adversary may be doing, and developing. That's what they were concerned about.

They told Paul, "Please keep in touch. We will work with you." And he thought, "Oh, okay, they want to know about aliens and why they're here." That's not what they wanted to know. They wanted to know why he was doing it, whom he was talking to, and what he was picking up on his instruments.

Mishlove: You mentioned another person, William [Bill] Moore, who is part of this story. How does he get involved?

Bishop: Bill Moore was a UFO researcher who wrote the original, *The Roswell Incident* in 1980. This was the book that started it all. He was a member of the APRO board who became interested in the case because the AFOSI [Air Force Office of Special Investigations] sent out letters to UFO researchers with a strange story about a UFO sighting on a military base. The reason they sent it out, Bill told me, was to find out who would respond and how they would respond to figure out if they were people they wanted to contact. Bill called the person named in the document and they said, "That happened, but it did not happen in that way. This document has nothing to do with what actually happened to me. I had a sighting, but all the rest of it is inaccurate."

Bill came back to the APRO board and said, "This is fake. There's no way to really check this out." But because he had actually checked it out and talked to people, Doty and people in the Air Force realized, "Okay, here's somebody that is thorough; they're circumspect, and they don't just take every story at face value if it conforms to their predisposed beliefs." They contacted him and said, "Could you please talk to, keep an eye on, and tell us who is talking about what things." They didn't tell him what those projects were. They wanted to know what UFO researchers were talking about. If the UFO researchers were to say, "I saw this big black thing take off from some Air Force base somewhere." Of course, somebody from a foreign intelligence agency would write to them and ask, "What was this thing you saw?" because it would be information they could possibly use. It wouldn't be some alien craft; it would be something the Air Force was working on.

Bill said a few other UFO researchers also accepted this deal. He claims they never paid him. I've known him pretty well for many years. I don't think they paid him but if they did, it wasn't very much. In exchange for the work he would do, they said they would give him UFO information from the government documentation. People are very interested in UFO documents from the government now. The AFOSI said he would have access to these documents and he got access to lots of them. Lots of them probably were fake or useless, as he told me later.

Mishlove: In other words, we're talking about the Air Force Office of Special Investigation. They were in effect infiltrating the UFO community.

Bishop: Yes, for information. People think that they were infiltrating because they wanted to mess with the UFO community or misdirect them or whatever. I think the misdirection would be, "You're getting too close to some sort of secret project. Here's some UFO information. Why don't you look at this aspect of it?" That would kind of steer them away from what they didn't want them to talk about, like a black project, and towards something else. It was not to make them disbelieve in UFOs or anything like that.

Mishlove: I would assume in the 1970s, 1980s, we're looking at the development of stealth technology.

Bishop: Yes, that was the biggest thing then. I've talked to people in the intervening years since I wrote the book, and the lights Paul saw taking off and going over the base may have been early drone technology. They look like glowing balls. Bennewitz said that he would look through his binoculars and see Air Force personnel at two in the morning walking around these things. Then they would walk away and the things would take off and move through the air. To me, it sounds like some sort of drone technology, but Paul thought they looked like UFOs. Who knows what those things were, but they were being tested on the base. I don't know why they were doing this right out in the open where people could see it. But they were doing this really late at night, so I guess they figured most people were asleep. But Paul wasn't. He was out on his porch watching these things.

Mishlove: And he had a great view.

Bishop: He had a perfect view, yeah.

Mishlove: And all kinds of telescopes, binoculars and electronic equipment.

Bishop: Probably spectrographs; things like that. He was also picking up radio transmissions that he thought were from an alien civilization. As far as I've been able to determine, the base personnel were testing microbursts, which is a type of technology that sends a lot of information in a very small amount of time. If you listen to it, it sounds like a tone or a "brrp" or something like that. It's basically coded information all shoved into the equivalent of a microdot, except it's an electromagnetic signal. Those were probably being used to control missiles or who knows what. Paul was starting to figure these things out because he was so good at electronics. He thought he could pull the messages out of these signals that he said were from alien civilizations on earth. He was trying to make the Air Force aware of this.

Bill Moore, for his part, all they told him was, "We will give you access to these UFO documents." They kept up their part of the bargain. "All you have to do is tell us what people are saying and what they're doing and who they're talking to and what they're talking about," which he did. He also did other things, too. They trained him to tail and investigate people. He became an unpaid spy for the Air Force for a while; he didn't just do UFO stuff. Bill lived in Los Angeles for a while and they had him track people down whom they were trying to find. He didn't go into detail with that for me.

The other thing that happened, which I thought was fascinating, was that Bill obtained postcards which were supposedly from Russian UFO researchers writing to UFO researchers in the United States. They said things like, "I'm interested in this case. Please tell me about it. Is there any news?" Just innocuous things. Bill would have to call a number, and it was always a different number. Somebody would answer the phone and say "hello" or something like that and he would read to them the contents of the postcards verbatim, including spelling errors, punctuation, everything. Then they would say, "Thank you," and hang up. He would also get instructions to take the postcard, put it in an envelope, take it to a specific post office and send it on to another address. I asked what those were and he said the Russians were sending out encoded information on missile factories and troop movements or whatever. It sounds like silly cloak and dagger spy stuff, but a lot of it worked like that. Apart from being a UFO researcher and helping the government, it was kind of exciting to be a spy, even if it was an unpaid one.

Bill developed a relationship with Paul Bennewitz. Because he's a member of the APRO board, Paul trusts him immediately. Bill basically just watched Paul, talked to him, kept an eye on him and got back to the Air Force about anything he'd heard.

Mishlove: Let me ask you, the Aerial Phenomena Research Organization is no longer in existence, to my knowledge?

Bishop: No, when the founders, Coral and Jim Lorenzen, passed away, it pretty much lost all its momentum. It's like a lot of organizations: when the original founders, the figureheads and the people that provide all the organization and the energy to keep it going, go or die or lose interest, it just falls apart. MUFON, the one that's still in existence now, split off from APRO. Walt Andrus founded the Tri-State UFO Study Group in 1967, which became the Midwest UFO Network in 1969. They still exist as the Mutual UFO Network.

Mishlove: I should point out for purposes of disclosure that when I was a graduate student at Berkeley, one of my dissertation committee members was James Harder, whom you write about in your book, who was the research director of APRO.

Bishop: They were an organization that prided themselves on having academics and scientists on their board and, yes, Harder was one of them. He figures in the story because Bennewitz asked him to hypnotize a woman who said that she had been abducted from northern New Mexico around 1978, 1979. She was steered towards him because somebody in the New Mexico State Police knew him as a UFO researcher and the most likely person to deal with her claim.

Mishlove: Who specialized in hypnotizing people who claim to have been abducted or claim to be contactees.

Bishop: Yeah, Harder did this. I believe Harder also was sent to hypnotize Travis Walton and the people involved in that.

Mishlove: That's correct, the Pascagoula case.

Bishop: That's Snowflake, Arizona. I think he also went to Pascagoula too.

Mishlove: He did go to Pascagoula, but I'm not sure about Travis Walton.

Bishop: I think he was one of the people that worked on the Travis Walton case too.

Mishlove: I'm not surprised. Back in the 1970s, when I knew him, he was one of the country's most prominent UFO investigators, along with J. Allen Hynek and Jacques Vallée.

Bishop: And one of the few people that did regressions along with Leo Sprinkle, who just passed away about a year ago. There were only a few people doing hypnosis then and Bennewitz happened to know Harder through APRO. Paul called him to Albuquerque—I think probably on Paul's dime, because he had this business—flew Harder out there and had him hypnotize this woman. A lot of details emerged. As you know, with hypnosis, people are very suggestible. Whatever the original story was and what had happened to her soon developed into this saga where what she said she saw connected with what Paul Bennewitz thought he was seeing. She talked about underground bases. He had become very interested in underground alien bases. Eventually his attention was directed toward the Dulce, New Mexico area, because the Air Force actually told him there was an underground alien base there. It took his attention away from Kirtland AFB, which was what they wanted.

Mishlove: The Dulce, New Mexico area is described in the book *Skinwalkers at the Pentagon*, recently published because during the AAWSAP [Advanced Aerospace Weapons System Application Program] period of research around 2008, 2009, 2010, one of the projects they looked at were all these strange sightings going on.

Bishop: The Institute of Discovery Science sent people out there. One of the people they worked with was a character in my book, Gabe Valdez, who was a New Mexico state policeman who had jurisdiction over that area and knew the Jicarilla Apache tribe. He started investigating cattle mutilations there in the 1970s when they had just begun. Bennewitz knew him as the UFO guy on the state police. Valdez drove this woman,

Myrna Hansen from Eagle Nest, which is in northeastern New Mexico, all the way to Albuquerque to meet with Bennewitz.

The reason they knew each other was because one of the senators from New Mexico, Harrison Schmitt, the astronaut, convened a conference in Albuquerque at the Central Library, in 1979 about the cattle mutilation phenomenon. He wanted to get to the bottom of it. Everybody that might know anything about it got together and gave presentations about what may have caused the mutilations. Paul Bennewitz met Gabe Valdez there because Paul was into the UFO side of things and Gabe was investigating the cattle mutilations.

Mishlove: Myrna Hansen is the contactee, or abductee, who, as I understand the story, eventually came to live in Bennewitz's home. He invited her to move into the house.

Bishop: For the period when they were doing the hypnosis, I think she did stay at the house. The way I understand it, Paul was there asking her loaded questions based on his ideas about what was going on in New Mexico and in the United States regarding alien invasion. That's what he thought was going on. The AFOSI encouraged him in his delusions because they wanted to hear what he was doing, but they also didn't want him to get near any secret projects.

In at least one case that Bill Moore was involved in, AFOSI made up a document for Bill to deliver to Paul. Bill told me he didn't want to do it. After a period of days or weeks, AFOSI said, "You do it or the deal's off." This is another spy tactic. He took this document, which has become known as the Aquarius document, to Paul's house. Basically what it said was the Air Force and the national security state was interested in UFOs and that there was a clearinghouse at Bolling Air Force Base for all this information including UFO information. They also mentioned for the first time ever, I think, that the information was under the purview of a group called MJ-12.

Bill took the Aquarius document over to Paul's Thunder Scientific office one night when it was closed and asked for Paul to meet him there. Bill told me that he asked Bennewitz, "Do you have a storage closet or something somewhere? Because I want to talk to you and I don't want anybody to hear." They went into the closet and Bill said, "Bring a radio." He turned the radio volume all the way up. He gave Paul the document and said, "I was told to give this to you. Take it with a grain of salt. Be very careful about what you do with this." Paul took it, and Bill said he put it in a safe and never mentioned it again.

But the point was that Paul read it and it reinforced his belief about how involved he was in the UFO investigation and how right he was about this alien invasion stuff. I thought it was very funny. Did you see *Confessions of a Dangerous Mind*, the Chuck Barris biopic?

Mishlove: No.

Bishop: Chuck Barris said he worked for the CIA as a hit man. Nobody knows if it's true or not. But George Clooney plays Jim Byrd, the CIA handler for Chuck Barris. In the movie, Byrd comes to Barris' house tell him something very important. He turns the stereo all the way up and yells in Barris' ear. The audience can't hear what is said, but there are subtitles. I was like, wow, that's exactly what happened to Bill Moore. It's straight out of the spy playbook.

All this cloak and dagger stuff was going on around Bennewitz. He thought it was that he was onto something important. The AFOSI, the NSA, any other agency that was around there, were happy to have him deluded as long as he could keep doing what he was doing, to build these maps of who knew each other. You know, "I am UFO researcher from Russia. I'd like to know ..." Well, you could check up on that guy and find out.

As far as I know, they busted a couple of spy rings based on some of Bennewitz's information. It contributed to finding people that had been embedded in the United States that were here to vacuum up information and send it back to Russia, just like the people sending the stuff on the postcards to Bill Moore. It was such a weird drama.

Mishlove: There's another wrinkle in all of this that we should explore. Albuquerque, which is a metropolitan community, has helicopters and small aircraft flying around all the time. I heard a presentation to this effect at a UFO conference a few years ago that if you factor all of that out, it seems that Bennewitz was *still* recording sightings of objects flying around Kirtland Air Force Base in Manzano Mountain that were not accounted for.

Bishop: That is a distinct possibility. The reason I say that is because there were some documents released sometime in the late 1970s, early 1980s that talked about landings at Kirtland Air Force Base. You can take it with a grain of salt, but they weren't really elaborated on. They didn't describe anything more than, "Something landed. Some guards got very nervous and then the things took off." It made government officials very nervous because it was right next to some nuclear weapons or storage facilities that would concern them, especially the Department of Energy who have purview over that kind of stuff.

The subtitle of the book is *The Story of Paul Bennewitz, National Security, and the Creation of a Modern UFO Myth.* Sometimes people say, "You're just trying to explain UFOs away." I say, "No, no, I'm trying to tell you that it involves the national security state and the UFO part was used for information, disinformation, and as a tool. It's like a tool in a toolbox. This doesn't mean there are no UFOs and no unidentified things. That's a separate issue.

Mishlove: It's a separate issue but this is a layer that has been going on for decades.

Bishop: It's still going on now. It's been going on very heavily in the last few years since that article came out in the *New York Times* by Ralph Blumenthal and Leslie Kean. When people ask me about that, of course, my brain is thinking about military intelligence. What are they interested in? Why would they want to do this? I go back to Bennewitz. They're not interested in UFOs. They're interested in what people think about UFOs and how it can be used to get information. Maybe even to find out about the UFOs themselves and see if there's some sort of technological or intelligence value in examining them and talking about the subject seriously on a public level. I think that article was a shot across the bow to crowdsource UFO research among people who are credentialed and have degrees and to take that UFO stigma away. That way they can get a lot richer information flow about what this phenomenon might be and how it might be useful or exploitable.

Mishlove: So, Bill Moore essentially became an informant for the Air Force Office of Special Investigations.

Bishop: Yes.

Mishlove: At the same time, he's a board member of the APRO organization at the time; possibly the largest UFO research organization.

Bishop: As Bill said, there were other researchers that had the same deal, but he wasn't at liberty to talk about it. It sounds like he's trying to push responsibility on other people. But it stands to reason that the AFOSI would get as many researchers on board as possible to help them out using various motivations— money, information, being a spy, whatever. It has nothing to do with making the UFO field look bad or getting them away from the truth. It's just a tool. The way Bill described it to me was one cog in a huge machine. I describe it that way to people as a giant clockwork mechanism with 500 turning wheels. The Bennewitz thing I wrote about is one cog in that giant machine.

Mishlove: Well, Bennewitz is a very interesting character because he's highly competent. He's managing a very successful high-tech business.

Bishop: Which still exists, actually.

Mishlove: Which still exists. He has a great view overlooking the Kirtland Air Force base and all kinds of equipment that enables him to monitor what's going on there. On the basis of his own observations, he's become convinced that we are in the midst of an alien invasion.

Bishop: Yes. And I'm pretty sure he came up with that idea on his own. But it was encouraged by the intelligence people who were watching him. Morris said he watched him get further and further away from reality. He said, "I warned him multiple times. Paul, you ought to back off here because it's affecting your physical health, your mental health, and your family." He just watched him get worse and worse. He said he went to lunch with Paul once and watched him light one by one, an entire pack of cigarettes and not finish smoking them. At a certain point, Paul's family got so scared about his mental state, they had him put in a mental health facility for about a month just to reset him. Apparently, it worked. He was out after a month or so and the mania had ramped down quite a bit.

There are scary parts of the story, too. Bennewitz said that somebody had come into his home at night and had injected him with chemicals. I asked a few people outside of the intelligence community, because intelligence people are going to tell me what they need to tell me, not necessarily the truth, and I realize that. I talked to people like Gabe Valdez and he said, "Yeah, I could see injection marks on his arm." I don't think Paul was doing it to himself. So who knows what was going on? That's a very sinister part that I never got to find out much about.

Bennewitz's family absolutely refused to cooperate with me, which made me uneasy about doing the book. I had to rely on friends, acquaintances, printed sources, things like that, and put the story together based on those sources to tell it chronologically. Bennewitz was a tragic, almost mythological character. He had his quest, but he had this Achilles heel regarding his belief system and would not check the information coming in. He filtered it based on his belief system; his mania just fed on itself and got worse.

Mishlove: His belief system was apparently reinforced by some of the Air Force officials with whom he interacted. Then the policeman, Gabe Valdez, introduced him to the abductee, Myrna Hansen, who was then hypnotized by James Harder at Bennewitz's home, I assume.

Bishop: He wrote about this in his document, "Project Beta," which is what the book is named after. He wrote, "This subject told us this kind of information. We had these protocols," but it was all predicated on: "There are aliens here and they're trying to take over the planet."

Mishlove: Hypnosis had become a tool often used to help evaluate cases of ostensible abductions going way back to the Betty and Barney Hill case.

Bishop: Yes, I think that was probably the first, at least as far as anybody knows; not just the major case, but [also] the first case where that was used.

Mishlove: 1964, as I recall.

Bishop: It's interesting because there's a whole mythology, idea, and scenario around UFO abduction now, but there wasn't then. They were flying blind and they basically had a similar scenario. It's fascinating because the Betty and Barney Hill story had no precedent but it matches current claims: cars stopped, people put into an altered state, beings taking them on ships, medical examinations, letting them go. Then it's recalled through hypnosis. That means there's something very important psychologically, if not objectively, going on there. We still don't know the answer to that.

By the time you get to Bennewitz, there's a protocol about how that should be. Plus, you add in Bennewitz's belief system: what he's trying to find out. I think that really affected her recall. So who knows what exactly happened to Myrna Hansen? She said that her car was stopped; she was with her son and they saw something floating over a field. She said she saw a cow standing under this UFO and getting floated into it. Somehow, she and her son ended up on the UFO and had the medical examination.

It is an interesting part of the UFO mythology that was amplified by Bennewitz's ideas about aliens. He was there the entire time while Myrna was being hypnotized, talking to her, and asking questions. When you're in a suggestible state, like hypnosis, your memories become very malleable and fluid. That's not a case to not use hypnosis but, as a tool, I think it may be inexact. The thing is that Myrna's recall was reinforced by Bennewitz and then in turn reinforced Bennewitz's ideas. I believe the underground base hypothesis started with Myrna Hansen because she said that at some point she saw this underground facility with military people present. Military abductions later became part of the UFO world, MILABs they're called.

Mishlove: It sounds like from what you're saying that a certain aspect of the UFO mythology—the MILABs, the men in black, the military underground bases and so on—a lot of that was generated by the government for purposes completely unrelated to actual UFO investigations.

Bishop: It was generated mostly by Bennewitz, as far as I can tell, but encouraged by the government people to get him to stop paying attention to Kirtland. They actually flew him in a helicopter to Dulce, New Mexico, and, as I was told, put props in the mountains that looked like jeeps, storage tanks, things like that, and said, "Look Paul, there's an underground base right here; you ought to look into it." They flew him up there twice to encourage him to go to that area.

The funny thing is that when I wrote the book, I thought it was just complete disinformation. I found out later from Gabe and others from the Jicarilla tribe, who I became friends with, that there probably was an underground facility, but who knows whether it had to do with aliens or not. Gabe told me he saw holes in the mountain with air coming out of them. There was something there, but as far as I can tell, it had nothing to do with a joint US government alien base or anything like what Bennewitz thought was there. But that myth was built upon and now it's a bedrock myth of the UFO community.

Mishlove: The Dulce, New Mexico area is even today reportedly a site of lots of paranormal activity.

Bishop: In the 1970s, when Bennewitz was first up there, people were seeing strange lights flying around; they still do, and they come in waves like a lot of UFO sightings. They were not aircraft, not even secret aircraft, and they were doing things that aircraft aren't supposed to do. They were the standard UFO sightings such as balls of light, things like that. And then, strangely enough, Bigfoot was spotted, too. There is enough Bigfoot activity that researchers go up there. The people in the tribe that I know have allowed me to take my drone up there to see if there were any Bigfoot nests or trails. It's a very pregnant area; pregnant with the paranormal.

The cattle mutilations occurred in Dulce, and [it] was one of the flashpoints for the cattle mutilation mystery that began in the 1970s. Gabe Valdez was the police officer looking into the mutilations. He showed me, and I think I put it in the book, that he got threatening phone calls. He also had electronic bugs in his house. He showed me pictures of them: one from when he had opened his phone up and found it inside. He had it examined. It was the type that picks up audio and rebroadcasts it. He said he had one in his smoke detector. He showed me that. If it's just aliens or a cult or whatever, why is somebody monitoring phone calls and threatening people around there? It's a whole other mystery too that is related to the UFO thing. But there's probably more evidence once there's a dead cow.

Mishlove: So, we've got many layers going on.

Bishop: It's such a wedding cake of all these different things.

Mishlove You've got the possibility of paranormal activity, however you want to define that. I think of it maybe as extra-dimensional interpenetration of our three-dimensional reality. You've got normal human psychology and all the foibles associated with just standard human activity, which includes an enormous amount of foolishness. You have the possibility of, we don't know if they're extra-dimensional or extra-terrestrial, but there are so many abduction cases reported and we don't know the basis of those yet.

Bishop: There seems to be an external source for a lot of these things, but we make assumptions because humans like to do that. You want to know what's going on. Evolutionarily, we have to know what's going on to survive, so we have to make sense of things. Even if it makes crazy sense, at least we've made some sort of sense of it. It's ripe for somebody like the AFOSI to put their own stamp on it and let people think, "Let's believe *this* about it." I'm not saying that's all UFO things, but when it has anything to do with the government, I think you have to be really careful about what they're telling you and about their information. "Hey, come over here. You're a good researcher. We're going to give you some information." And then you just become a repeater station for whatever kind of disinformation they want to throw out.

Mishlove: Well, they may have been concerned for all we know about foreign spies infiltrating UFO organizations.

Bishop: They were very concerned about it and that happened. Bill told me he knew a UFO investigator from China named Paul Dong who had written a book about Chinese UFOs. The AFOSI asked Bill to befriend him and keep an eye on him. Bill told me that Paul Dong had an acupuncture business in the Bay area along with his wife. Bill knew he was working for the Chinese government and Paul Dong knew that Bill knew this. It was this weird kind of gentleman spy agreement. Bill would report what Paul Dong said, what he was doing, where he was going, what his ideas were. It's this spy game that goes on all the time. It's just that, once in a while, it intersects with the paranormal and UFOs.

There are people in the government that are genuinely and sincerely interested in this just like we are. They figure they can use their connections to find more information. Bill is a member of this group, which became known as The Aviary. He and his research partner named it that. But they were just people in the government.

Mishlove: Curious people.

Bishop: Yeah, curious people. Hal Puthoff and John Alexander were the two most famous people in the group. They would meet informally every once in a while and find out from each other what their government contacts had said. They were almost like a civilian research organization except they all happened to have security clearances. Bill had some sort of low-level clearance so he'd be able to talk to these government agency people.

But it's so strange to see these people doing basically what UFO organizations do but at a different level. It's a human interest and it's always going to be. They will use it as a tool if they need to.

Mishlove: Bill Moore, as you describe in your book, at one time went public at a UFO conference and confessed that he had been an informant for Air Force Intelligence.

Bishop: Yeah, and he was vilified for it. What people didn't realize was that he didn't have to say anything. He didn't have to admit this to people. It wasn't that he wanted attention. Who wants negative attention? Who wants everybody hating you? He said he did it for several reasons. First, he asked the powers that be that he was working with, "Is it okay if I talk about this?" They said, "Yeah." I guess they said not to mention certain things. There were already rumors going around that he was a spy except the information was all completely wrong or inaccurate and he wanted to put that to rest. And, most importantly, he wanted to warn people that if government people came to them and gave them special information, to be very careful.

As I said in the book, it's the best speech I've ever seen because of the audience reaction. They had to stop the talk. This was in MUFON in 1989 in Las Vegas. I had met Bill about two years before. He said, "I'm going to blow their socks off." "What are you going to talk about, Bill?" He said, "I can't tell you. Just come to Vegas, help me sell books, and you can see what happens." Vallée was there. It's the first time I met Jacques Vallée, I think, was at that conference. So he saw it, I'm pretty sure. Bill was the keynote speaker and had the premier spot on Saturday night: the one they want everybody to see.

Bill goes up to the podium. It's a packed house, standing room only, and he starts talking about what happened: talks about Paul Bennewitz, about Doty, as much as he could about the entire operation. I reveal more in the book. As he starts speaking, people start yelling. If they had brought things to throw, they probably would have thrown things, too. It was very emotional. I saw a woman crying. People left the room. The state MUFON director had to call for order more than a few times.

When he was done with his keynote address, instead of taking questions from the audience, he asked his own questions and answered them, which made them even more angry. I asked him why he did that. He said, "If I just asked people for questions, it would have been pandemonium. I couldn't have answered the questions. I knew what was going to happen." When he was done, he said, "Thank you and farewell," and he walked out the back door next to the stage and disappeared. It was a shock to everybody, because he basically confirmed all these rumors that the UFO field had been infiltrated by intelligence people. He even told them the reasons he did it. But they focused on, "Why did you do this? We trusted you and you betrayed us." The real betrayal would have been saying nothing. But he did say something; he talked about it.

I'm very biased toward Bill because he's a very good friend of mine. People say, "Why do you believe all this? He could be lying to you. He could be part of this government disinformation." I said, "Two reasons. One, he's a friend and, two, I've never caught him in a lie on anything. He will tell me things and I'll find the truth out about it days, weeks, months, sometimes years, or even decades later." He's never steered me wrong. That's hard to convey in a book because people don't know your friend.

Because Bill admitted it, we got very good insight into why government entities are interested in the UFO subject and how they use the information. Most UFO people chose to focus on what a horrible thing he did, not about the mechanics and procedures of the intelligence program. UFO researchers have been contacted over and over since then. I was contacted by a guy in the Navy who gave me secret information. He made me extremely paranoid for a while to the point where I couldn't sleep. I was looking out the windows. I thought people were monitoring my calls. It was terrible. They can do this to you, and they appeal to your ego. It's like, "Wow, I must be important if somebody in the government's talking to me."

At that point, they continue feeding you information. And, as I said, you become a repeater station. You just spit out what they tell you. In fact, I was told to put a few things in my magazine but I interpreted the information. I said, "Well, you can take it this way or that way." The guy got very upset with me because I hadn't just repeated what he told me.

Mishlove: Now, I didn't mention for the benefit of our viewers that you published a magazine. Since you brought it up, let's just cover the dates and the name.

Bishop: I want to give people a personal view of how this intelligence thing works and how it happens over and over again. I started a magazine called the *Excluded Middle* in 1991 with a couple of friends of mine. It covered UFOs, conspiracies, psychedelics, consciousness, and parapsychology. At some point, a friend of mine said, "There's somebody I know who wants to talk to you." The contact used the name Mike Younger. Apparently, there are a group of people in the Navy, he told me, that are naval intelligence. I said, "Why naval?" They said,

"Who do you think has the purview over most of the earth? The oceans are the Navy. So they have a much wider net where things are seen." And of course, strangely enough, the *New York Times* article was about Navy flyers.

Mike Younger approached me with pictures of UFOs at Area 51. He gave me all kinds of documents and information, supposedly inside information, because he said, "We think you're doing a good job." They just wanted me to spread their information, or their disinformation. I didn't do it properly, so eventually they dropped me, which was fine. Being a spy was interesting for a while. But he told me things like, "People can listen to your phone calls. They can see what's on your computer screen." This was in the mid to late 1990s. "They can open your mail," which I had mail opened, Jeff. I went to the post office and found mail that was obviously opened or "destroyed by postal machinery". The destroyed mail was from two people: an abduction researcher, Karla Turner, and a cattle mutilation researcher, Peter Jordan. Nothing else was touched at that PO Box for my magazine.

I got phone calls all the time where the phone would ring—this was before cell phones—I would let my phone ring 30, 40, 50 times before they would hang up. If I turned the answering machine on or picked up the phone, all I would hear was electronic noise or nothing on the other end. After a while, a terrible paranoia built up in me. Eventually, I just got tired of it and decided to stop feeling scared. Many UFO researchers are strung along this way and they spit out whatever is told to them, which is exactly what the intelligence agencies want. It doesn't bring us any closer to answering the mystery. To me, it's just noise.

Part of the reason I wrote the book is to warn people that this has happened before, and it will happen again. It is an intelligence agency model that is successful because it is useful and it relies on human psychology. They flatter your ego by telling you something that other people don't know, and saying that you've been chosen to spread these things. It's very easy to get this disinformation, or modified information out. It's designed to lead people away from things or toward things for national security or whatever the government's working on that's secret.

I'm more interested in what causes UFOs, not this other stuff. There's a way to winnow out information that isn't very important and concentrate on the phenomenon itself, how it affects people, the history of it is, and what we can do in the future with it.

Everybody's life seems to have a story. I think Joseph Campbell said that when you get near the end of your life, you see this narrative. That's kind of how I feel about this subject. I started out being interested in everything. Then I got narrowed down into the government stuff. Then I realized that's not really telling us anything about this subject that we all love, that we really want to find out more about. Here's a little filtering tool. You can ignore this part, or pay attention to it because it might tell you something interesting, but concentrate on the phenomenon itself, the people involved with it, and how it affects them. That will tell us more about that mystery.

Mishlove: Greg Bishop, what a fascinating conversation. I know we're just scratching the surface of your vast knowledge. I'm delighted that you're here with me in Albuquerque. Thank you so much for being with me today.

Bishop: Thank you.

11

The UFO/UAP Disclosure Process
with
Daniel Sheehan

J**effrey Mishlove:** Hello and welcome. I'm Jeffrey Mishlove. Today we'll be exploring the UFO disclosure process. My guest is Daniel Sheehan. He is the author of *The People's Advocate: The Life and Legal History of America's Most Fearless Public Interest Lawyer*.

For the last fifty years, he has been active in some of the most prominent cases in American history: the Pentagon Papers, the Watergate burglary, the Karen Silkwood case, the American Sanctuary Movement case and the Iran Contra Affair. He represented psychiatrist John Mack when being investigated by Harvard University, due to his interest in alien abduction cases. Daniel is currently heading up an organization called the New Paradigm Institute. They will soon launch a new initiative to hold Congress responsible for UFO (Unidentified Flying Object) and UAP (Unidentified Aerial Phenomena) transparency. Dan is located in California. Welcome, Daniel. It's a pleasure to be with you today.

Daniel Sheehan: Thank you, Jeffrey. It's a pleasure to be here.

Mishlove: We'll be talking about the whole UFO disclosure process. It's a very hot-button issue right now with the whistleblowers. You've been involved in the UFO arena, at least, since John Mack was being investigated by Harvard University. So you have a long history already working in this area; plus your caseload reflects many, many other areas involving social justice. I guess you see this as an area that's consistent with your other work, in the social justice arena.

Sheehan: Oh, absolutely. But it's important to remember that I first became involved in this back in 1977, almost twenty years before John Mack. That's one of the reasons John called me. He asked me to be his lawyer, while I was at Jesuit headquarters. I was general counsel at the United States Jesuit headquarters, in their social ministry office, developing public policy. President Carter's people first reached out to me. They were preparing a classified report for him on UFOs and extraterrestrial intelligence. I became involved in it from a spiritual context, and having to do with consciousness—and its potential impact on human consciousness. My involvement with this subject came from that perspective, because of the role consciousness has in social justice.

Mishlove: That makes perfect sense. If I recall correctly it was the United States Library of Congress that Carter had tasked to prepare the report and, so, they called on you.

Sheehan: That's right. It was the Congressional Research Service, the Science and Technology Division of the Congressional Research Service tasked to do the study. Marshall Smith, the director then, reached out to me and asked me to participate as special counsel.

Mishlove: How did the report go, incidentally?

Sheehan: Well, it's interesting. It kind of descended into a statistical study, a mathematical computation of Drake's equation and the probabilities of discovering other life elsewhere in the universe. And, remember, at the time the scientific community in the academy didn't even officially acknowledge there were other planets outside of our solar system. Pursuant to the scientific, logical, positivist worldview, the thinking was until you measure it and weigh it and taste it and feel it, it doesn't exist. And so they weren't acknowledging any other planets. The people doing the study resorted to statistical work, measuring the number of star systems and the likelihood of how many planets there were around them. It was all probability projections.

When we began to talk about concrete evidence of actual UFO contact, it became more problematic. When I discovered photographs of the UFO crash retrievals, and I was given access to classified portions of Project Blue Book, I ended up bringing this evidence back to Jesuit headquarters and providing it to the headquarters' files. Then we reached out to the other fifty-four major religious denominations in the United States. We asked them to put together a task force to try to get ahead of this theologically. They didn't do it. So it was an interesting period back there in 1977, when I first began working on this subject. I realized, once I'd seen the photographs and I knew that the UFOs were real—I had always assumed they were and I'd always anticipated they were real. Once I saw the actual photographs of a genuine UFO, in the custody of the United States Air Force inside their classified documents, I turned my attention to trying to get this (disclosure) to happen. I've been at it now for forty-six years or so.

Mishlove: That's amazing. You actually saw those photographs, had them in your possession, [and] shared them with the Jesuit ministry back in 1977?

Sheehan: Well, technically what I did is, I traced them. They refused to allow me to take any photographs out of there. I just opened up the yellow pad and I traced the actual symbols on the side of the dome of the spacecraft recovered. I brought those drawings to the headquarters. When I did, I gave them to Father William Davis, my immediate Jesuit superior; I was a candidate for the Jesuit priesthood at that time When I gave the drawings to him, he opened up his desk drawer and took out an envelope. He handed it to me. I opened up the envelope. Inside was an 8.5" x11" black and white glossy photograph of a UFO. I said, "Wait a second, where did you get this?" He said, "My sister Dodie gave it to me." And I said, "Well, where did she get it?" He said her husband, Mike, an air traffic controller at the Seattle airport, got it from his best friend. He was a pilot that took the photograph out of the window of his plane. He didn't want to get in trouble for fear of losing his license. So he took the photo to the air traffic controller, his best friend. He, in turn, didn't want to get in trouble either. So he took the photo and gave it to his wife and said, "Here, take this and give it to your brother. He's a priest."

Mishlove: What a fascinating story. It highlights the bigger issue that's coming up now: the U.S. government, it seems, has had in its possession for decades, maybe going back to the 1940s, various crashed alien craft.

Sheehan: That is right. The first one that I'm absolutely certain about is the July 1947 crash debris from Roswell. The reason that I'm so confident is when the United States Air Force lied about it, saying, "Oh, no, no, we don't have any craft here, there's nothing to see here," a famous photograph emerged, taken of General [Roger M.] Ramey. He was the commander with supervisory authority over the 509th bomber squadron, who recovered the craft. In the photo, he was kneeling next to a faked up weather balloon, sitting on the floor. He had in his hand a telegram of some sort. You could see it in the photograph.

In 1995, while I was representing John Mack, someone approached me saying they discovered the photographer from the local Roswell newspaper that took the photograph. He was going to go to try to find him and see if he had the negatives. So I arranged with him, if he could get the negatives, I could possibly have them digitized. We could then blow up that telegram to get a look at it, and we did it. We were able to generate a digital reproduction of the telegram. It said right on the telegram, "Take the saucer to Wright Field and bring the victims with it." It said that. And so I knew from that point on, not only had I seen the actual photographs of a crash retrieval but [also] I now had proof. There was this telegram from Roswell acknowledging the saucer was real and that it had bodies with it.

Since that time, I've been able to be among the people where ... For example, when I was representing Dr. John Mack and became legal counsel for his peer group, the Program for Extraordinary Experienced Research [PEER], I interviewed dozens and dozens of people who had direct, face-to-face contact with extraterrestrials. I've been able to discern, after having done hundreds of depositions in my life as a trial attorney, who the credible witnesses are. I have tons of credible witnesses I've interviewed. I've seen photographs of the crash sites. I've helped to participate in viewing the telegram that General Ramey had in his hand at Roswell. I'm among those people completely convinced that it's all true: very important when you're engaged in the discovery process. It's one thing to speculate while looking for information, to decide what you're going to think about something. I know the UFO stories are true and, therefore, I approach it with that kind of confidence. When I'm interviewing people or I'm investigating, I'm doing it from the point of view, not from an experiencer, because I've had no direct contact. I haven't even seen a UFO except for in photographs. Yet, I'm sure that it's true. And now the Congress of the United States is acknowledging it.

Mishlove: For sure something is going on. The question is what? Amongst all of the reports, obviously there's the question of craft that have actually been retrieved and bodies that have presumably been retrieved. Then there are reports from people who claim they've had, as you just mentioned, face-to-face contact with alien beings. Then follows the questions of

UFO abductions and hybrid children and does the U.S. have a secret space program with our own starships? Have we already succeeded in acquiring the technology for these vehicles? There are still many, many open questions, at least in my mind.

Sheehan: Yeah, there are a number. For example, we've encountered a number of frauds where people want to come forward and pretend they know things they don't know. We've had certain individuals come forward saying they're part of a secret space program. They've been to distant galaxies on our starcraft and all that. I actively do not believe them. I don't believe these statements to be true. What they've done is taken some of the verified data—I think they've discerned a certain algorithm within the evolving facts then projected into the future—and then, they've asserted these facts are true. I don't do that. I take it as far as the evidence actually supports, at any given time. I insist upon doing the investigation, which New Paradigm Institute does.

We've set up a 501(c)(3) institute, the New Paradigm Institute, to undertake the investigations of UFO related incidents we haven't yet been able to verify. We've been intimately involved, too, with the process of trying to get the current piece of legislation passed. We can then work directly with the various congressional committees to get the information directly to them. The new UFO law, that's in the process of being passed right this week, basically, as we talk here, is going to move this forward to some extent. We must continue this operation, on behalf of our citizenry to get the information and gather credible stories. There are lots of photographs now. There are many tape recordings. There are other things we can bring together to make the case. As a practicing trial attorney, I have done a number of major cases, from representing the *New York Times* in the Pentagon Papers trial, to being the people who filed the federal, criminal racketeering charges against the off-the-shelf enterprise of Oliver North. And, like the Karen Silkwood case, that caught the CIA smuggling bomb-grade plutonium to Israel and to Iran, we have proven it in court. We've done all these cases. We want to bring this same level of expertise to these UFO investigations. We're hoping to have a receiving audience at the Congressional level to present this information. And, of course, we've been in direct communication with a number of whistleblowers who have come forward from deep inside these secret programs. Government crash retrieval programs and reverse engineering programs; we're getting Congress to listen to the people involved to decide what to do.

Mishlove: Let's talk about the legislation that is now pending. I believe we're referring to the Defense Authorization Bill, which is huge.

Sheehan: 3,930 pages. The section that we're talking about was the 24-page amendment we wanted to insert into the National Defense Authorization Act. It is basically the UFO Controlled Disclosure Act. I've tried to set up an independent panel that was going to be reviewing all of the information that the U.S. government has in its possession. Very importantly, they would be armed with subpoena power to extract the information from: the Central Intelligence Agency, from the Defense Intelligence Agency, from all eighteen of the United States intelligence agencies, all six of the military services, [and] all thirty-two of the Defense Department agencies. Most importantly, from private military contractors, who have possession of some of the technology recovered from these UFOs. They're using it to try to develop a super weapon system. It's like the old Sufi saying, "When a pickpocket meets a saint, all he sees are his pockets."

What has happened is that the Defense Department officials, those capturing these saucers, immediately start thinking how they can transform the tech into weapons. They're missing out on the extraordinary. There's a story that Hal Puthoff told me—Hal has been involved for a long time in working on these things, as you know, you know, Hal—he said that when he was talking to the science advisor for President Clinton and was asking him, "What have they got? What are we going to be able to do with this?" The science advisor said, "Look, let's go outdoors and take a walk here and let me talk to you." And he went on, "Let me give you an example of what I think is going on. Let me tell you a story." There's this story of an old man walking home early one evening. He's walking through a field and he sees a little light in the grass. He bends down and sees that there's a frog in the grass. And it's got a light on its head. He picks the frog up. It turns out that it's a crown on the head of the little frog. And the frog starts talking, saying, "I'm really a princess. I've been turned into a frog by an evil sorcerer. All you have to do is kiss me and I'll turn back into a princess. You and I will be married and you'll have the whole kingdom. We will have many children together." The old man looks at the frog and says, "... well, actually, I'm at an age where I think I'll settle for having a talking frog." And he took the talking frog home.

And so, that's the story Hal tells. It's about the possibilities we're passing up here, at least temporarily, to have direct, open communication and access to this extraterrestrial civilization and to understand what an additional billion years of evolution might do to the phenomenon of consciousness; or answers to the fundamental questions we have, both theological and metaphysical, involved with the UFO phenomenon. It is this extraordinary opportunity that's facing us. You and I and those of our generation, have another twenty to twenty-five years to devote to this subject. We need to make use of the time. Bring this information out to the public, on our watch, at least in this incarnation. I'm hoping, in my next incarnation, to be a starship captain. It's probably not going to happen this time around. So I play this role, trying to do this good work.

You spent time working on the areas of consciousness and wrote about the extraordinary, metaphysical types of experiences that people have with the UFO phenomenon and occupants. I'm very interested in this aspect of the whole thing, but also in dealing with the legal implications of it all. Legislative steps we need to take—investigatory steps, the recovery of the craft, etc.—is an entire spectrum of issues. All are at play in the UFO phenomenon. Our generation wants to address all of it to help future generations to understand the phenomenon.

Mishlove: I'm pretty sure a lot of people figure this could be a military threat to us. If the aliens, with their advanced technology, want to interfere with our way of life, there is very little we could do to stop them. So from a military point of view, it would seem important that we understand their technology.

Sheehan: As I said, when a pickpocket meets a saint, all he sees are his pockets. The fact is, if we have a set of structures that include a standing army, like George Washington warned us against, we have an army whose obligation is to take a certain narrow perspective on the issue of our national security. For example, look at the 1992 United States Defense Department policy planning guidance documents. They were prepared under then Secretary of Defense Dick Cheney. They state, specifically, our mission is to seek out and maintain continued privileged access to the strategic raw materials needed by our major corporations. The DOD views this as their operational mission assignment. So it's not just that they're trying to defend us. What they're trying to do is, in their own words, [to] establish the full spectrum of dominance over the planet. And they say so, right, in these documents. They view it as their mission statement. It's not just trying to figure out how to protect ourselves against this new UFO technology. What they're trying to do—and we've discovered this—is trying to back engineer the tech to build a missile system to deliver thermonuclear weapons in a warhead, launched from United States territory, to hit Russia or China, within two minutes.

This is a serious challenge. As people devoted to trying to elevate the consciousness of our human family, we are attempting to take out of exclusive hands the dealings with this phenomenon. It must get it into the hands of Congress. We have to get it into the hands of the churches. We have to get it into the hands of the economists and sociologists. We have to get our whole human family, all of the disciplines, involved. Over the centuries, we must continue—and bring this phenomenon forward, so as to have a holistic approach rather than a narrow-minded military defensive, or dialectical confrontational perspective.

Mishlove: I don't know that we're going to be capable of changing the American military structure, although if anybody is up to the job, it's probably you. I know that the National Security Act goes back to the 1940s. The creation of the intelligence community, the CIA and that whole network harks back to then. They've all been well established since before I was born.

Sheehan: December of 1947, the National Security Act of 1947 created the Central Intelligence Agency. The thing to keep in mind is the agency was created at the direct behest of one of the senior partners of Brown Brothers Harriman, a coalition of robber barons attempting to monopolize resources. Robert Lovett is the guy that wrote the memo to President Truman, asking to create the organization. The CIA views themselves as being operatives, too; basically, of a certain kind of economic prowess. They want to assert themselves over the world. That we have to change. It's absolutely appropriate as long as there are nation-states.

I studied under Henry Kissinger at Harvard College of Foreign Policy. I know what the implications are of the present nation-state system. It's confrontational, it's competitive, and in fact, they attempt to establish ultimate military superiority over every other nation-state. They do it under the rubric of defense. But when it devolves into an offensive capability, the United States, for example, our military budget every year— they're just getting set to approve in the National Defense Authorization Act this December '23—is ten times bigger than any other nation in the world. In fact, it's bigger than the top ten of the other nation-states in the world, all together. We keep on insisting this is for defense purposes. But we have 800 military bases all across the world. We're insisting, China is asserting control over the South China Sea and is interfering with our national security.

We've brought into NATO the republics released by Gorbachev. At Jesuit headquarters, we were in direct communication with Gorbachev, trying to talk him into stepping back from the Cold War, to disarm the nuclear warheads, etc. As soon as he stepped back, the US Defense Department, under Dick Cheney and George Bush, Sr., tried to move in to fill the vacuum and establish full-spectrum dominance over the planet. They said so. There's a job we have to do to get our citizenry to actually elevate our collective consciousness. We must try to get the instrumentalities of our government to reflect a higher state of consciousness. Or at least move our military back to a legitimate defense posture, and out of this offensive posture they're now in. It becomes directly pertinent with regard to the UFO issue. They're trying to use the technology to develop this offensive weapon. It's a first strike weapon. The code name for the program is called Prompt Global Strike.

Mishlove: I understand that the government would be interested in exactly that: a prompt global strike. I'm not at all convinced there's a link between that and UFO technology. I could be wrong. Of course, I have very little direct information. My best sense is this technology is so far advanced, above anything that we have, even though governments and private organizations, businesses presumably, have been attempting to reverse engineer this stuff for decades, [but] haven't gotten to first base with it.

Sheehan: Well, I'm afraid they're on first base. They haven't hit the home run yet, I believe, but they're on first base. The fact of the matter—take a look at what they're doing. Radiance Technologies, for example, is developing this Prompt Global Strike program. This super-fast missile developer has hired people right out of the Defense Department: specialists in UFO technology. That's what they've done. So you know perfectly well, that's what they're still doing. They've been negotiating with Lockheed Martin to get one of the spacecraft. They can then work on it to promote their rocket technology.

The two congressmen that have shown the greatest resistance to this bill, which we tried to get passed, are right from the Redstone rocket missile testing range in the 2nd district of Alabama. The Wright-Patterson Air Force base is in the tenth district of Ohio. These are the two major people organizing the resistance against passing the bill giving greater disclosure of UAP/UFO information. They want to keep it secret and they want to have patents. They want to have patents. They can make literally trillions of dollars in mastering the anti-gravity and the superluminal propulsion systems. That's what they want. They realize the major money to finance and develop both of these technologies is in the weapons industry.

We name this, at Jesuit headquarters, sinful structures. We have sinful social structures in place right now. Pedro Arrupe, the superior general of the Jesuits when I was in the order, asked all of us, all the Jesuit priests, to engage in daily work to disassemble the sinful and unjust structures that abide on our planet. It's not a matter of attacking individuals or attacking even personal integrity. The people are part of the institutional structures in that they accept mission assignments from our structures. These are potentially destructive of the entire human family. We all know we live under the umbrella, every day, of potential thermonuclear destruction. And yet, we haven't been successful in getting them to disassemble those weapons. We've got to do that.

Mishlove: In fact, if anything, they'll make bigger and stronger weapons if given a chance.

Sheehan: That's right. Not even given a chance. They'll take the chance. That's what the problem is. They're not under constitutional control. They're supposedly in authority, like anybody in the government, as delegated by the people. And the fact is, we have not delegated that kind of authority to them. They've taken it on themselves. They've kept it secret from the elected representatives. They keep this secret from some elected presidents. Even secretaries of defense haven't been briefed. That's a problem we are trying to overcome.

Mishlove: When we spoke earlier, we talked about the unacknowledged special access government programs and that the policy is, if somebody, a reporter, should question you about these programs, it's perfectly appropriate to lie.

Sheehan: That's right. And to Congress, to lie to Congress, to lie under oath to Congress, to lie to your president, your commander-in-chief. In fact, even within their own juridical structures, they think they're authorized to lie. They view elected representatives as temporary employees of the government. They view themselves as a permanent institution of the government. The fact is they tend to think of *themselves* as the government. These are military people and covert intelligence people. They view themselves to be in charge of the government. It's totally untrue. It may be true in a dictatorship. It may be true even in some communist nations, but it is not true in a democracy. They haven't been adequately trained or conscientized to understand the difference. We have to exercise our authority as citizens, not only to help our country, but [also] to help our whole human family. We're the five percent of the population of the entire world that can actually have a direct effect upon the policies of their government. We have to do so. It's an obligation that we have. It's a spiritual obligation, in my opinion.

Mishlove: Well, at the same time, it does seem that a lot of information is coming to us about UFOs; about aliens. In fact, a great deal of detailed information comes through the public sector. For example, individuals claiming they've been aboard these craft. Some individuals claim they were given access to pilot some of these vehicles. And the vehicles operate not on a technology that we think of as technology, but by consciousness, and when you're piloting, your thoughts become important.

Sheehan: That's right. That is true. In fact, in the Roswell crash in July of 1947, one of the technologies was removed from that craft, according to Colonel Philip Corso, in charge at the Pentagon in July of 1947, and he was charged with the recovery and analysis of foreign technology. He was put into possession of the helmet that was worn by the pilot of the crash saucer in Roswell. It was clear that the craft was navigated by telepathy. In fact, I've talked with another witness who believed he came upon a UFO craft. He was hiking in the mountains of Colorado on his summer vacation from college. He called me and asked me to come and see him. He didn't want to reveal his name as he is a famous person. He said he walked right up to a UFO sitting in a meadow. He went over and he put his hand on it. He could tell that it was alive. The technology of integrating consciousness into a machine is what's going on with AI right now. They're actually using human stem cells. They put them into computers to generate dendrites and synapses from the human brain. If you add another billion years to the time to develop this kind of technology, it's possible some of these UFO craft actually have sentient capacities. They interact with the telepathic communications of the pilot.

Now, these are the kind of things that you wouldn't have dared talk about 10 years ago, even if you did know it. But, today, we know perfectly well of the secret programs inside the Pentagon and the Central Intelligence Agency. Both are exploring this issue: what is the unique relationship between consciousness and the UFO phenomena? They know that there's something going on there. Hal Puthoff and his people have been directly involved in trying to explore some of that information. That's why the churches are important, too. They must realize, all religions of our human family, have to do with human consciousness. We have the capacity to discern other dimensions, other vibrational dimensions of reality. And so this is an extraordinarily rich field.

Really, we need to be able to persuade the academy, the universities, to begin exoplanet studies to really understand what the UFO life may be like. What may their culture be like; what changes our culture has to go through in order to accommodate a relationship with a culture like that. This is the next step. We've mounted a major campaign to get the legislature and the government structures involved in sharing the information. We must do the same with the academy, with the universities and the churches and the synagogues and temples. We've got to get our whole human family, all of our institutions, moving into a new era here. So that's what the New Paradigm Institute is doing.

Mishlove: Well, you've got a tough job ahead of you. I know as a graduate student in parapsychology back in the 1970s, I did research on an individual who seemed to have telepathic contact with aliens; could make UFOs appear on demand. There are many examples of that and even today there are people still doing that. I had a professor, a parapsychologist, someone very open to psychic functioning, drop off my committee because he said we cannot mix the science of parapsychology, which is struggling for acceptance, with another crazy fringe science like UFO investigations. They must be kept separate because otherwise we'll be laughed at. Of course, we're laughed at already. So it's going to be a very tough road when the different people investigating paranormal phenomena don't even want to talk to each other.

Sheehan: I know. It's a challenge. There's no doubt about it. I was one of the people involved in the State of the World Forum. At the end, I pointed out that our Jesuit office was in direct communication with Mikhail Gorbachev. We were working on him to step back from the Cold War; getting him to sign the Concordat, and releasing provinces from the Soviet Union. We were attempting to draw people into a conversation about what a new paradigm, worldview would look like. That is, if we weren't engaged in a dialectic confrontation with the Soviet Union. During that time, the Jesuits convened the State of the World Forum with Gorbachev attending and US Secretary of State James Baker participating, as well. We invited various world leaders.

It was there I met Dr. Zhenzhou Jing. Dr. Zhenzhou Jing was from the Chinese Academy of Social Science. It's a huge university complex in Beijing that is at the disposal of the Politburo in China. She was in charge of the Science and Technology Division. She invited me to come to China. The first thing she did when I arrived was to show me the laboratories where they were working on psychic issues and psychokinesis. She showed me the videotapes of Uri Geller, and other psychokinesis things. That was back in 1999. That's 25 years ago. China knows what they're doing in this area.

One of the first things I talked about with Gorbachev, when I was alone with him, was the UFO issue. We know that the Soviet Union has been working [on this]. But we can't allow this as some kind of competition. They're trying to build weapon systems or weaponize the capacities of our human family. We've got to back up out of the process. Only by the people such as yourself and others, who are willing to undertake certain courageous actions, [such as] getting the University of California at Berkeley to allow you to do your PhD studies on psychic phenomenon. I've been confronting the same issue here. I was able to get the Jesuit Order to support this and to authorize me to deliver a three-hour, closed-door session with the Jet Propulsion Laboratory. We discussed the SETI program and the theological implications of contact with an extraterrestrial civilization. They're the ones that authorized us to reach out to the Washington Interreligious Staff Council. We asked fifty-four religious denominations to set up a task force in an attempt to get ahead and understand this subject.

There are some institutions supportive of this. I've had conversations with Johan Ickx, the head of the Vatican Archives. I tried to get access to the archives for research purposes when I was at Jesuit headquarters. We have to—those of us who are familiar with the authority of institutions in our human family—to get these institutions to move. We cannot be confined to only what is authorized information, at any given point in time. We have to have the courage to organize our citizenry into a collective community. We must reach out and do this on our own.

That's why reaching out for telepathic communications with extraterrestrials is important. Do the CE5 activities by going out into the fields at night and making yourself open to these contexts, and try to prepare so that you are not cellularly terrified when in the presence of one of the UFO beings. They are so very different from us. Our entire cellular system of self-survival may recoil, at the first encounter. I've talked to dozens of people. No matter how well prepared they thought they were, when it happens, their entire body freezes up. It will take time to get used to these beings. So we've got work to do. And I'm glad that you're still at it. I know I'm going to keep at it. I've got another twenty to twenty-five years before I would consider retiring. But I will never retire from this effort.

Mishlove: Let's talk more about the defense authorization bill and the amendment that is currently in the bill that relates to disclosure. What outcome can we expect?

Sheehan: Well, as a university professor, I'm used to figuring out how to grade my students. I would give it about a 65. It's passing, but I'm not going to write a letter of recommendation to grad school for the work done by the Congress. It will set up a framework. It does, in fact, issue an order from the Congress to the CIA and to all six of our military services, all eighteen of the United States intelligence agencies, all thirty-two of the defense agencies, and to every one of the aerospace technology corporations in possession of technology. Tech that should be turned over to the National Archives, so the people with security clearances will be able to get access to some of the information—except there is no enforcement device. There's no subpoena power. There's no punishment for refusing to comply. But it's an important sign that Congress, even the House of Representatives, where they were resisting this most, have agreed to the order.

The problem is, when I was chief counsel that put forth the federal, criminal racketeering charges against Oliver North, we succeeded in getting Congress to pass the Boland Amendment in 1984. This prohibited the Reagan-Bush administration and the CIA and the military from providing any type of military support, direct or indirect, to the Contras. They were declared, by an International Court of Justice, to be criminals, and were to be prohibited from any military aid. So Congress issued the order prohibiting our agencies from doing so. They went right around them. They insisted upon going ahead and doing it themselves. They consider themselves to be the government. And so they were providing weaponry to the Contras, to the deposed Sandinista dictator, Anastasio Somoza.

And we caught them doing it. While working through the church, Jesuit headquarters, we presented it to the judicial branch. Finally, we forced the legislature to hold public hearings on their actions. But the bottom line is no one was ever punished for it. No one. Out of all of the drug smuggling, all the political assassinations, all of the weapons violations, nobody was ever prosecuted. The bottom line is, without enforcement mechanisms, the national security state people take it unto themselves and refuse to obey the law. They view themselves as being above the law. They won't respond to this new law. But we know they'll have to give some information over to the national archives, and some of it will be made public.

Our New Paradigm Institute is going to be gathering the information. We have offices right on Capitol Hill. We're going to be able to go over and get the information out of the archives. We're going to be able to put it into a form the people can understand and explain the full implications. We're going to do this. So the new statute will provide some assistance in this whole endeavor. We don't want people jumping out of the first story window of their house, and then having to dust themselves off and pick themselves up, in despair over the inadequacies of the bill. What I've said is, the glass is partially full and partially empty. I won't say half full. I wouldn't give it a full. But it may be half full and half empty. Our job is to focus on the part that's still empty and help fill that in. If they don't respond, then we do it ourselves as citizens. After all, this is still a self-governing country. We have the capacity to do it if we can get people to pay attention.

That's one of the reasons why we have to have the New Paradigm Institute. The information needs to get to people in bite-sized, digestible forms so they, in between football games and basketball games, and the women now, too, will pay attention to this issue. And we're winning. There are more and more shows on the Internet about the UFO issue. There's a weekly series of programs talking about all of this. One of my number one jobs for the New Paradigm Institute is to try to curtail some of the more bizarre, crazy, conscious lying that goes on. Also, we have to try to get *Ancient Aliens*, for example, to adopt a more rigorous standard of proof: more so than some ancient alien theorists believe. That's not the right standard. Some believe that President Clinton was an ET walk-in. Some of them believe that Biden is having secret, face-to-face meetings with extraterrestrials. We have to get rid of that. We have to put the lie to that type of information. It needs to get taken out of the discourse. I'm not in favor of censorship, but what I'm saying is, we construct affirmative structures, such as this on your show. The key is to use discretion with whom you interview and whom you put on the air, thus acting as a voluntary filter for credible information.

That's one of the things we want for the New Paradigm Institute: to be viewed as a source of solid, credible information about an otherwise non-credible subject. It's an incredible subject, this issue of UFOs and extraterrestrial civilizations. But it's growing in credibility. We will invoke the assistance of Congress to give it more credibility. We'll invoke the testimony of whistleblowers from inside to give it more credibility. We'll invoke the *New York Times* to give it more credibility. We'll invoke *60 Minutes* on CBS to give it more credibility. We'll give it to Jeffrey Mishlove, of the New Thinking Allowed Foundation webcast to give it more credibility. That's what we're doing at the New Paradigm Institute.

Mishlove: I think one of the important factors is this is a nonpartisan issue. You've got a lot of support from both sides of Congress to push for this and overwhelming public interest in having disclosure, as far as I know.

Sheehan: That's right. There's virtually no legitimate opposition to this except from the forces that are trying to keep it secret. Those making very dangerous weapon systems out of it. Otherwise, there's no reason in the world not to discuss the subject. It's not true that the churches are pushing back against it. Many say, "Oh, well, the churches are not going to let you talk about it because it's going to destroy their religion." That's not true at all. I was the legal counsel in the headquarters of the largest, single denomination, the largest order of that denomination in the world. The Jesuits are supportive of doing this. I need to do more work, to get them to be a little more forthcoming. They've still got information in the archives that Johan hasn't let me see yet. I'm still working on it. Father Jose Gabriel Funes, for example, was the previous director of the Pontifical Observatory. He's now teaching a class down in Argentina on the theology of extraterrestrial contact, all with the full sanction and support of the Catholic Jesuit order.

So there's a process going on here. I'm hoping to accelerate it. We all are helping to accelerate it. We're going to be doing some of that ourselves at the New Paradigm Institute. We will try to construct, as part of the plans, a curriculum for an undergraduate degree, a bachelor's degree in exo-studies, a master's degree, and a PhD program. We've been offered a full facility one hour north of San Francisco, up on Clear Lake. There's a 70,000 square foot old art deco hotel we can use as a base for providing bricks and mortar instruction. We also have an online university with accredited degree granting authority.

We're going to be doing these things to help raise the consciousness of people while training people in an academic field that is pertinent to them. Whether relevance to the individual comes from economics or geopolitical strategies or theology or philosophy. This is an extraordinarily exciting period. We're privileged to live at this point in time. This is a pivot point of history, for our entire human family. We're going to be stepping out into the stars now. We will realize that we are a part of a large, galactic civilization. Even though we may no longer consider ourselves at the apex of the pyramid, of all sentient life in the universe. We once got over this fact: we are not the physical center of the universe, during the days of Copernicus and Galileo. Now we need to get over this, too. We can't despair and think we don't have value.

In the matrix of conscious life in the universe, we need to understand what our value is. What is it about the human family we can contribute? I don't think it's necessarily the capitalist economic system. I don't think it's the military state. Hopefully, there are some higher achievements we've accomplished and can share. It's extremely exciting.

Mishlove: Earlier you used the phrase—well, I introduced it when I said I didn't think they've gotten to first base in terms of back engineering a UFO—you said, you thought they haven't hit a home run, but they probably are on first base. I wonder if you could elaborate on that.

Sheehan: They've had access to this for some time, since at least back in 1940s. They've been devoting a lot of time and attention and lots of money to these experiments. For example, I talked with Edgar Mitchell, when he was still alive, and he said one of his best friends was actually in a laboratory where they were trying to figure out anti-gravity. They're working on the anti-gravity stuff. They've actually been able to develop some kind of primitive technology that alters the weight of objects. At that time, they hadn't gotten to the point where it would levitate. The fact is, however, they could place an item on a scale, and could subject it to technology that would reduce its weight by one half.

He's also been at a place—and this is a big one—where in one room, and they put a Coke bottle, I don't know why they picked the Coke bottle, for the example, other than the fact that it's kind of archetypal. They had a Coke bottle, and put it on the table. He put a little tag on it, writing his signature on it, too. They had him go into this other room, and he waited there. He heard this kind of weird noise. Suddenly, a light started to appear on the table. Then the Coke bottle manifested from the other room, with his signature and stuff on the bottle. So they're experimenting with this kind of teleportation thing. This may have something to do with the way the UFO vehicles move from one star system to another one, without having to just travel super-fast. We know they've been doing this.

And we know that in the mid-1950s, *Popular Mechanics* and *Scientific American* were filled with cutting edge experiments going on in the areas of anti-gravity and other stuff. Then all of a sudden, it all disappeared. Abruptly, they stopped doing any news articles about the topics. We know it then went underground, and the United States military moved in to take control of the research. And we know, now, they have this missile in the Prompt Global Strike Program that, apparently, can travel at mach-25. That's not normal technology. That's not just putting a little more fuel in it, or burning fuel, burning petroleum at a little more efficient rate, or any other thing. They've obviously begun to cut into the new technology.

There are some who believe there are even more advanced technologies. They believe they're on at least second base. Dr. Steven Greer is one of the people insisting he has talked with others who have given him, what he believes to be, convincing information. There is some type of operational craft they can pilot. They have been experimenting with this out in New Mexico. Steven and I have had this long—and I was general counsel for his disclosure project for twenty years—we've had calm and centered discussions about this topic, always, and are still good friends. But I've now started to represent Luis Elizondo, and some of the people from inside these programs. So we're getting more and more information about these crafts.

But I've refused to risk a security clearance. I absolutely refuse. If I were to do that, I'd then be prohibited from talking to people about what I know. And the fact is, if I haven't proven it yet, I will prove it. I'm capable of getting at virtually any information that's around, because I offer a sound and reliable place to bring the information to. That's what we have with the New Paradigm Institute. We're going to have trusted people involved: all being capable and responsible. We are going to push the envelope to get more and more of this information made available.

I do think you're right. They've begun to develop some of this technology, but it's still, I think, in a fairly crude state of development. We have to get a treaty put in place. We have to get a treaty where the United States will take the lead and say, look, we're willing to put all of our technology on the table. Please stop trying to develop any other weapon system. Everybody has to agree to do this, too. But the nation-states that are in the lead are the ones that must initiate this action. Otherwise everybody's saying, oh yeah, you're only advocating for that because we've got one better than you've got.

I think the time is now. We've got to get President Biden to agree. Let's get Jake Sullivan and the folks to put this on their agenda, to take the next step ahead. I've talked with other candidates about this, and they really need to start getting this on their agendas. They're still afraid a big taboo remains about even talking about UFOs, because of the success of the secret programs, and what's going on inside the CIA. They attempt to totally destroy people; destroy their careers, destroy their family lives, if they try to reveal any of this information. We've proven that.

Richard Dolan, a PhD candidate at the University of Pennsylvania in history, has written two volumes titled, *UFOs and the National Security State.* He's got internal documents showing the CIA and the Defense Department had a criminal covert operation going on, destroying people, [and] destroying their lives and their careers, if they tried to reveal any of this information. It even went so far as regular civilians, who had seen a UFO or had direct contact, to prohibit them from talking about it.

The problem is that there's still an overcast on this issue of ridicule and fear. Actually, of being able to talk about the subject. We have to try to get over that. That's part of the responsibility of the New Paradigm Institute. We must start making it a part of our regular discourse, and regular courses of instruction. What are the economic implications of this? What are the scientific implications? What are the theological implications? We've got to get it down into an everyday kind of conversation before we can make the full progress we need.

Mishlove: How can our viewers be of assistance to you?

Sheehan: The most important thing they can do is just go onto our website—it doesn't cost anything; it's totally free—come onto our website, newparadigminstitute.org. You can find all the email addresses for your congress people and your senators. They should still be doing this between now and December 21st, to keep telling their senators and congress people they want full disclosure. They want full responsible disclosure. That's the first thing that they can do.

The next thing they can do, of course, is dig further into the website and find the information. What is it that makes it credible now? Why is it that the United States Senate made official findings that they knew that our government was in possession of information about possessing a craft like this? Why did the House Intelligence and National Security Subcommittee of the Oversight Committee hold public hearings telling the world that we had this craft? We need to share this information. They can come onto the website, www. newparadigminstitute.org

for lots of this information. We have documentary films. We have scientific studies there.

Our job is to make this information entertaining, interesting, engaging, not some pedantic kind of lecturing of people. We're going to try to get major motion pictures made that are not fictional, that don't go off the deep end like Project Blue Book did on television. When they had Dr. Hynek seeing UFOs, finding bodies in cellars and all that stuff, none of that's true. Stick with the facts. But they're still exciting, dramatic, and entertaining. That's our job at the New Paradigm Institute.

It's also professionally responsible, in the fields of economic studies and academic importance, to bring these studies into the academy. That's one of our major missions, to bring the subject matter into the academy; to get the new generation trained to have an entirely different consciousness.

Mishlove: I am under the impression that this policy of discrediting the witnesses is no longer in effect. It's just a vague impression I have, based on recent revelations. Do you know any more about that?

Sheehan: Well, it's interesting. It's clear that at least some people inside the national security state infrastructure haven't gotten the office memo on this yet. They're not supposed to be doing it. For example, people don't realize this but David Grusch's testimony, on July 26th of this year [2023] to the House Oversight Committee, was completely authorized by the Defense Department's pre-publication authorization process. Lou Elizondo and Chris Mellon, when they brought the videos to the *New York Times*, all of that was cleared. There's activity going on inside the national security state structures of authorizing some of this information to come forward.

But still, there are others inside the Defense Department establishment, the intelligence establishment, that are retaliating, as David has testified. He and his wife received threats from them. Lou Elizondo, they were threatening to take away his security clearance. The same thing with Christopher Mellon, even though they've been officially authorized to say it. So the memo hasn't been gotten by everybody inside the national security state. We think that the more we are public about all of this, the deeper the memo is going to go into those circles.

The real problem is with the private aerospace industry. They have private security companies. Have people watch *Michael Clayton*, the movie that Participant Productions did, that shows the lengths to which private security companies will go. When we did the Karen Silkwood case, for example, the Kerr-McGee Nuclear Corporation had a private security company working for them that actually ran Karen Silkwood off the road. They killed her because she was trying to bring to the *New York Times*—David Burnham was waiting for her at the *New York Times*—and killed her to silence her. There are people that believe resorting to violence is okay still, to silence the people. We have to overcome that. We have to not be afraid.

But I'm saying that there have been steps taken to try to silence Lou Elizondo, to try to intimidate Chris Mellon, [and] to threaten Dave Grusch. But they're holding fast. They're not being intimidated. They're continuing to go forward. They're taking all the steps to make sure the things they say publicly have been authorized. The whistleblowers, for example, we have about forty of them lined up inside the Senate Intelligence Committee. They don't trust the AARO office, the All-Domain Anomalies Resolution Office. They view AARO as a replay of Project Blue Book. They're just trying to capture whatever information the whistleblowers have and kill it and keep it secret. They don't trust them. We have to improve the performance of the AARO office.

But the fact of the matter is that until we get the people to stop threatening our witnesses, they're going to be afraid to come out in public. So we're offering legal representation. The New Paradigm Institute actually provides legal defense to some of the whistleblowers, like Lou Elizondo and others. We will provide that service to others, as well. We will do our best to explain to those that are threatening others that it's not to their advantage. Let's put it that way.

Mishlove: Daniel Sheehan, you have a long track record of standing up against organizations that are some of the most outrageously evil in the world. It's not a term I would use lightly. So I think if anybody has a track record, a portfolio of the sort of experience required to take on a task like this, that has been secret for so many decades and is now slowly coming into public awareness, you're the guy. I look forward to future conversations with you. You're welcome to come back to *New Thinking Allowed* over and over again. I gather that you're a vortex of information. I'm happy to be able to work with you to make as much of this information public as possible.

Sheehan: Terrific, Jeffrey. I definitely appreciate that. We will have a number of these conversations.

Mishlove: Great. Thank you so much for being with me today, Daniel. It's been an eye-opening experience and a joy and pleasure to be with you.

Sheehan: Terrific. It's mutual. Thank you, Jeffrey. Thank you so much.

Mishlove: You're welcome. And for those of you listening or watching, thank you, because you are the reason that we are here.

About the Author

~

New Thinking Allowed host, Jeffrey Mishlove, PhD, is author of *The Roots of Consciousness, Psi Development Systems,* and *The PK Man.* Previous books in the *New Thinking Allowed Dialogues* series include *Is There Life After Death?* and *Russell Targ: Ninety Years of ESP, Remote Viewing, and Timeless Awareness.* He is the recipient of the only doctoral diploma in the world from an accredited university that says, "Parapsychology." It was awarded from the University of California, Berkeley, in 1980. He is also the Grand Prize winner of the Bigelow Institute essay competition regarding postmortem survival of human consciousness.

The New Thinking Allowed Foundation has recently launched a quarterly magazine. Copies can be downloaded for FREE from www.nta-magazine.magcloud.com and you can also order high quality print copies as well.

Milton Keynes UK
Ingram Content Group UK Ltd.
UKHW030827010824
446326UK00004B/168